THE GREATEST
CURIOSITY

The Unlikely Adventure of a Texas Oilman
Navigating the Russian Oil Business

— JEROME M. FULLINWIDER —

The Greatest Curiosity
The Unlikely Adventure of a Texas Oilman Navigating the Russian Oil Business

Note: Certain Russian names have been changed for privacy reasons.

Printed and bound in the United States.
Produced by: Epic Bound, LLC

www.EpicBoundBooks.com

ISBN: 978-0-692-34588-7

DEDICATION

**I would like to dedicate
this book to….**

…my Russian colleagues,
without whose help and friendship
I never could have succeeded.

…to my wife, Leah,
who stuck with me during long absences
and an uncertain future.

…to my children and grandchildren,
hoping that this book will further their
investigations into their own
greatest curiosities.

Table of Contents

Foreword

Even today, I'm amazed at the twists and turns my life has taken over the past twenty-some years.

I've always firmly believed that God has a plan for each of us, but I never would have guessed that his plan for me would involve working and living in Russia. I loathed its Soviet system, but I came to respect and admire its people. And isn't that what makes life such a blessing?

I LIKE TO THINK SO.

"I never would have guessed that God's plan for me involved Russia."

THE ITCH

1989 WAS A DISMAL YEAR FOR OIL.

Exxon made headlines when its tanker Valdez ran aground and spilled 11 million gallons of crude oil into the Prince William Sound off the Alaskan coast. The price of oil, which had taken a turn down in '85, was still in a steady decline. And in West Texas, where I lived and operated my oil business, V-F Petroleum Inc., new wells continued to come up dry. The thrill of drilling a large oilfield seemed a distant dream.

"It was time to retire to a beach, but it wasn't in my blood to call it quits."

I was almost 65, and, up until that point, had done reasonably well with our oil company. In 1964 aged 36, I'd made the leap to become an independent oilman and moved my family to Midland with only $5,000 in the bank (equivalent to $38,000 in 2014). With my partner Vic Vasicek, we successfully capitalized on our contracts with several major oil companies who had departed West Texas for richer pastures. In doing so, we carved out a niche and slowly succeeded where others had ceased to compete. Logic dictated that it was now time for me to check out and retire to a beach somewhere.

But it wasn't in my blood to call it quits. In fact, I was itching for something new.

Jerry Fullinwider at his desk in the Midland office, 1993.

A Simple Phone Call

My Russian adventure started, like many life-changing events, with a simple phone call. It was 1989, and at the other end of the line was Tom Russell, a charming and brilliant geophysicist. Two years earlier, I'd turned to Tom and his team at Professional Geophysics, Inc. (PGI), with a seismic problem that our West Texas consultants had difficulty with. PGI unraveled the mystery after six months work and sent me a bill for so little I was almost embarrassed to pay it. Recently, I'd heard that Tom had formed a new firm, MD Seis, which was pursuing the first U.S.-Soviet joint venture for oil exploration and production. In fact, I'd been forewarned that

Tom wanted my company to welcome a group of high-ranking Soviet oil and gas officials to discuss declining oil production in Russia.

I may have been looking for a change, but this was one offer I was prepared to decline. Meeting with Communists wasn't on this native Texan's bucket list. Every cell in my body loved free enterprise, but Tom was no dummy. He went after the two vulnerabilities he knew I possessed: curiosity and competition. He told me the names of the four other independent oil companies he'd invited to meet with the Soviet delegation. All were valued at more than

"Meeting with Communists wasn't on my bucket list."

$1 billion, or some 500 times the value of V-F Petroleum.

I still wasn't moved.

"Listen," I told him, "You've piqued my curiosity, but you know what I think of that miserable country. Why would I go anywhere to meet a bunch of damned Communists?"

I proceeded to wax lyrically a while longer about Communists and Communism. Although I hadn't flat-out said "no," when I finally stopped talking to listen to Tom's reaction, I felt confident he'd gotten my answer.

Then, he put his invitation in a way that I couldn't refuse.

"Jerry, I've done you favors in the past, right? So do me one back. Come on down to Houston and have dinner with these people."

When I hung up the phone, the first thought I had was "Great guns, what would Dad think of this?"

Remembering Dad

At pivotal moments in my life, I've often thought of my father, "Fully." A dedicated company man who served for a decade as president of Southern Ice & Utilities, Inc. in Dallas, Texas. He died suddenly from a heart attack when I was only 18. Although he wasn't around to witness my adult life, or counsel against many of my seemingly risky decisions, I knew he was always with me in spirit.

He did, however, get to watch my first "business venture" in the form of a popular swing band I started in high school. Playing jazz with friends started out as a fun hobby, but before long, I advertised our services — billed as The Southernaires — to other schools and social events, and the play dates came rolling in all over northeast Texas, Louisiana and Oklahoma. My parents were supportive, although I'm sure my Dad would have had a few choice words for me while I continued to prioritize music gigs over studying when I moved on to Southern Methodist University in 1946.

After graduation in 1951, however, I said goodbye to my band mates, and shifted my attention to serving our country, which was embroiled in the Korean War at the time. I sincerely felt called to serve, but I knew my

"I abandoned law for a more risky career—oil."

talents could be utilized in many important roles within the armed forces, not just firing a gun on the frontlines. After graduating in 1953 from the U.S. Naval School of Justice in Newport, Rhode Island, I was assigned to a position in the naval legal system away from the immediate action. At first, I worked with the court marshal defense teams and surprised many by my determination in getting the defendants acquitted. My acquittal rate was so good, in fact, that it didn't take long until senior officers recognized my success would be better utilized (from the Navy's standpoint) as a member of the prosecution teams. I excelled there as well.

After Naval Service, my life could have proceeded in the legal field — I would have been set if I'd gone on to attend a good law school and then open a private practice. But I quickly abandoned that plan in favor of a more interesting, albeit a bit more risky career field — oil.

After my Navy discharge, I returned to a position with Standard Oil (Ohio) in 1953 and later moved on to Cherry Brothers of Dallas in 1957. After learning the ropes from a few of the seasoned oil veterans in the state, I risked it all and attempted to go it alone as an independent oilman in Midland in 1964.

I'm sure my conservative father would have advised against some of my career moves. But working with Communists? That, no doubt, would have topped Dad's list.

Even I had to wonder what I'd gotten myself into now by accepting Russell's offer to meet with high-ranking Soviets.

Jerry Fullinwider.

Following in the Footsteps

In no small measure, my dad was responsible for my belief in free markets.

When I was a teenager, I'd sometimes catch a ride home with Dad from his office at Southern Ice. While he was working overtime, he once flipped me a pamphlet and said, "Read this, it's the new law of the land." What I read filled me with concern. It was the Wagner Act, a pro-union piece of legislation signed by President Franklin D. Roosevelt in 1935.

My dad was fighting to protect the interests of Southern Ice against the changing times. And in the days and months that followed, I grew to understand how such policies put a huge strain on my dad. His fight against unions may have been the fight that killed him.

But make no mistake; my dad's strong belief in economic capitalism was rooted in more than simple, unrestrained profit. It was a conviction, homegrown in Texas, about inherent freedom.

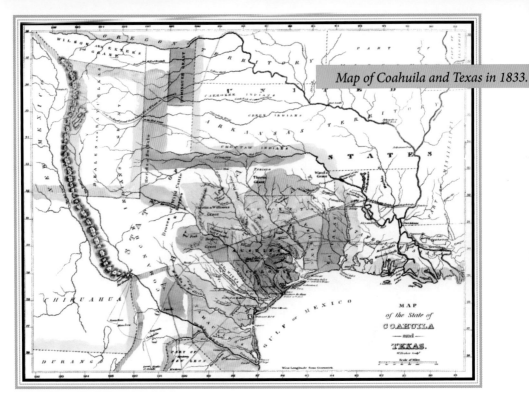

Map of Coahuila and Texas in 1833.

Long before FDR and the Wagner Act, a Fullinwider ancestor dedicated his life to bringing freedom in the form of the Protestant faith to the Mexican-controlled Tejas Territory in the 1830s. The Rev. Peter Hunter Fullinwider, a graduate of Princeton Theological Seminary, was the first Presbyterian missionary to defy Mexican President Santa Anna's edict that residents of Texas should practice the Roman Catholic faith.

As a kid, I listened with admiration to tales of this "old ranger" who travelled by horseback, stopping only to preach God's word and sleep under the stars. I used to wonder how he must have felt as he first headed into uncharted territories to fulfill what seemed like an impossible mission. And after Tom Russell's phone call, I'd begun to understand.

Certainly, if Peter Fullinwider could preach Presbyterianism in Mexican (Roman Catholic) territory, I could take the risk of meeting with a group of Soviets.

By the end of his life, Rev. Fullinwider had not only established several churches and was a founding trustee of Austin College, then located near Huntsville, he'd played a role in the birth of a state, earning himself a place in history.

Little did I know, by agreeing to attend Tom's meeting, I was just starting to embark upon my own unlikely journey into the history books as one of the first independent oilmen to do business in Russia following the collapse of Communism.

"If my ancestor could preach in Mexican territory, I could meet with a group of Soviets."

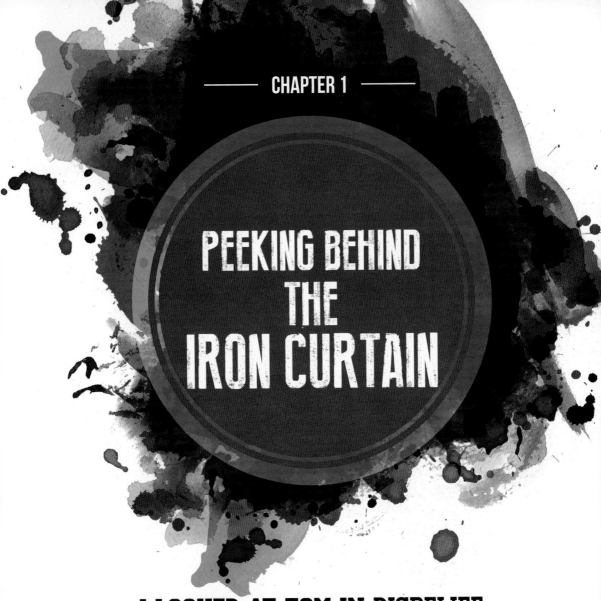

CHAPTER 1

PEEKING BEHIND THE IRON CURTAIN

I LOOKED AT TOM IN DISBELIEF.

"Holy smokes, you mean nobody's here?" I asked, incredulous. "We're alone?"

None of the big-player oil firms that Tom had invited to The Houstonian Club showed up for the dinner meeting with the Soviet delegation. The firms cancelled last minute, Tom explained; they would send a jet to Houston in a day or two to pick up the delegation for meetings in Dallas and other cities.

"Don't talk politics or religion and while you're at it, stay off sex."

— Tom Russell

Meeting with the 13 Soviets on this night would just be me and my politically like-minded friend from Dallas, Ilya Mamantov. Ilya was a retired geologist and a strident anti-Communist. As a child, Ilya had fled from Russia to the United States with his family who had fought against Lenin's revolution and lost. I had invited Ilya because I didn't trust these guys with whom we were about to dine, and I wanted him to translate precisely the words we would exchange with the Communists, whom Tom insisted were oil experts and not members of the Communist party.

As Tom briefed me on his expectations for the evening, I surveyed the guests — nine men and four women all dressed in black. With their black suits, black ties and white shirts with splayed collars, the men looked like undertakers, or maybe gangsters from the 1930s.

"Now, Jerry," Tom began. "Don't talk politics. Don't talk about religion. And while you're at it, stay off sex."

"OK, OK," I told Tom, trying to move things forward, so I could get this mistake of a dinner meeting behind me.

13

Tom called for everyone to take their seats that were designated by place cards. Tom sat to my right. On my left sat Dr. Nikolai Sevastianov, the head of the delegation, a tall hulk of a man whose huge head was covered by a towering shock of white hair. His hands were extremely large — big enough to crush grapefruits, two at a time. To his left sat Ilya, my interpreter. Tom went around the table and made introductions. Immediately following Ilya's introduction, the giant Russian wanted to know why Ilya was at the dinner.

"We don't need interpreters," Sevastianov said, seemingly offended. "In Paris, London and New York, we meet many oil groups and they don't have interpreters, ever. We have our own people here who speak good English."

"I'm sure that's true, Sir," I replied immediately. "But I'm a native Texan and an unapologetic capitalist. In fact, I'm anti-Communist and…"

I felt a sharp pain on my right leg. It was Tom, kicking me under the table. "Don't talk that way," he whispered loudly.

I ignored Tom, not missing a beat. "…I have seen all the 007 James Bond movies and read the spy novels, and I know how KGB interpreters work. I don't want any of yours filtering what I say to you, or what you might want to say to me.

My friend Ilya is here to keep the table honest."

I glanced over at Tom, whose face was now about 10 shades redder. I'm not sure if he was angry, embarrassed or both.

The Soviets seemed to enjoy my impromptu remarks; they erupted in loud laughter, which caught me by surprise.

"Meet Maj. Georgi Bogdanov, KGB," Sevastianov said, pointing out a man sitting three seats to my right, who smiled and waved.

"Just call me George," the spymaster replied.

I had, inadvertently, broken the ice.

For the next four hours, the Soviets, Ilya, Tom and I enjoyed steak dinners while we traded jokes, stories about our respective lives and tales from the oilfields. Here I was, a West Texas independent, a political ultra-conservative, and a died-in-the-wool Presbyterian sitting with the top oil people of the Evil Empire — and enjoying every moment.

My curiosity in overdrive, I had to force restraint. I wanted to know every last detail of who these people were, what they wanted to know about the American oil business — and why they wanted to meet with me.

"I've seen all the 007 movies and read spy novels. My friend is here to keep the table honest."

But I didn't want to pry too hard. After all, Tom and I were the hosts, and this was an occasion for getting acquainted over good food, much drink, amusing stories and quiet gauging of one another.

At one point during the dinner, Ilya came over to me and whispered that the Soviet interpreters, who indeed worked for the KGB, were accurate and honest, and I could believe what they say. I nodded and thanked my good friend for flying to Houston with me.

Throughout the dinner, I found myself drawn to a top official named Dr. Georgy N. Gogonenkov, a distinguished geophysicist, oil specialist, First Deputy Director of the Central Geophysical Expedition and a fluent English speaker. He was an extraordinarily pleasant and gentle man with twinkly blue eyes, white hair and rosy cheeks, and we hit it off immediately.

All or Nothing

During the meal, I had the opportunity to speak with many of the officials that evening and even though I had been warned about avoiding the topic of religion, I honestly could not help myself.

During my research on the Soviets I was surprised to discover information about President Gorbachev. I asked Dr. Nikolai Sevastianov, the delegation leader, "Did you know that Gorbachev was baptized in the Orthodox Church and raised in a Christian home in the Stavropol region in southern Russia? In fact, to this day, Gorbachev's mother still has a home altar where she prays for his safety." Just as Russell was recoiling his foot, ready to kick me, I continued, "Dr. Sevastianov, I want you to know that I pray for your president as well. I know he has made some good changes for your country and I pray that he will continue to successfully lead your people."

With that I let the conversation drop. Not sure if I had caused damage or found a way to share my genuine feelings and prayers for his leader. I decided not to push it any further, but as I turned my gaze away I could tell I had hit at something deeper with Dr. Sevastianov. The dinner continued.

"I pray your Gorbachev will continue to successfully lead your people."

Minutes later, Dr. Sevastianov clearly wanted to get something off his chest. He asked for everyone's attention. I could tell he was unusually animated, if not agitated.

As if a gladiator preparing for battle, he began extolling the virtues of the Soviet Union, which everyone believed would not likely survive much longer. It was a strange and stressful time in the world, and I could only imagine what it was like for these Soviets to face such an uncertain future given their charge to help improve it through expanded oil production.

He began by saying, "When I was a young man, like President Gorbachev, I too was baptized in the Russian Orthodox church. I learned about God and the importance of faith. And just like Gorbachev, my mother also prays for me on a daily basis."

This was an interesting and unlikely statement made by this man, as faith was not commonly discussed in this way.

He stood up as he talked, and as his speech continued he was more intense and emotionally involved. The whole crowd sensed the importance of the moment and was mesmerized.

"In the Soviet Union, we have the biggest hydroelectric dams in the world!" Sevastianov loudly proclaimed. "In the Soviet Union, we have the biggest army in the world! We have the best steel! We have the biggest steel mills in the world!"

Gripping the table, as if to hold himself from some kind of supernatural launch into space, he became loud enough to make me want to cover my ears.

"I myself have great prestige. I have my own automobile, my own driver, my own apartment with two bathrooms, and my own *dacha*." ("*Dacha*" is Russian for "second home in the country.")

"And my country's development charges ahead. The Soviet Union is always moving onward and upward. We have the best space ships! We have the best submarines! The best rockets! In the Soviet Union, ,,, vee haf vee haf…"

At that he slammed his great hand so hard on the table that I thought he'd surely broken it. The crash made everyone flinch, and caused some glasses to tip over.

"Vee haf… NAHTHING! NAHTHING!"

The room fell into silence; it was as if time stood still, a real-life scene from a Hollywood blockbuster.

"Nahthing, vee haf," he thundered again to the frozen room.

No one moved their startled gaze from his face. The hush persisted a few more moments. Then, slowly returning to the present moment, Sevastianov sat down and composed himself.

"Maybe," he said in almost a whisper, "Vee belief in God again."

It was unquestionably the most dramatic moment of my life. One that not only fostered a deeper connection with this group of delegates, but also instilled a sincere desire to see their country succeed. With faith in God, all things are possible.

"VEE HAF...
NAHTHING!
NAHTHING!
MAYBE,
VEE BELIEF
IN GOD AGAIN."

— DR. NIKOLAI SEVASTIANOV

Drinks with "Friends"

Sometime after midnight — three hours past the time I had expected dinner to end — our waiter brought out the last bottle of Armagnac in the club. The Russians had literally emptied The Houstonian of the stuff.

Finally at 1 a.m., we all rose to leave the table — but only because we had exhausted the entire supply of Armagnac. The empty bottles were lined up like cups on a sideboard. I couldn't have imagined such an enjoyable evening. I saw each of the 13 Russians not as a collective group of strangers unworthy of trust, but as individuals whom, one day under the right circumstances, I could call friends.

As I was preparing to leave the dining room where we had just finished the dinner that I thought Tom had arranged to pay, the head waiter brought me the check. Tom was nowhere in sight (a specialty of his). Dinner was going to be on me.

A SPECIAL KIND OF BRANDY

I knew Russians liked vodka. What I didn't know before that night is that they also love brandy — a special and expensive type of brandy called Armagnac.

"Our waiter brought the last bottle of Armagnac. I soon realized dinner was going to be on me."

Studying the Soviets

Almost immediately after I had agreed to travel to Houston for the first meeting, I began studying up on the Soviet Union — mainly, I confess, to help prepare the arguments I would offer in defense of capitalism, should the Communists start criticizing America.

What I learned from my research neither surprised nor disappointed me. The Soviet economy was near ruin following years of heavy investment in its military buildup at the expense of domestic development. The failed attempts at reforms, a stagnant economy, and the defeat of the Soviet Union's forces in the war in Afghanistan had led to a general feeling of discontent, especially in the Baltic republics.

Gorbachev's unopposed ascendancy to General Secretary of the Communist Party in 1985, following the death of Konstantin Chernenko, did nothing to stop the economic decline. To the contrary, his push for political and social reforms — along with some rushed and ill-advised shifts in economic policy — worsened the faltering economy, creating an atmosphere of open criticism of the Communist regime.

When the price of oil declined sharply in 1985 and 1986, a price drop that also hit the U.S. oil market hard, the Soviet Union suddenly found itself with no money in the state banks to buy needed grain or imports such as meat and sugar that were needed to manufacture basic food supplies. The country flirted with disaster. By the end of the 1980s, severe food shortages led to the reintroduction of wartime rationing, which required Soviet citizens to use food cards, limiting them to a certain amount of product per month.

The rationing may help explain why on one trip to Houston, members of the Russian delegation were delighted when — at their request to see U.S. capitalism in action — I took them to a Kmart store. You've never seen a happier bunch of people shopping the blue light specials.

They selected small items that they couldn't get back home, but could carry in their suitcases — kitchen utensils, candles, anything electric, small toys for children and grandchildren, and the like. The final tab totaled around $4,000. Of course, they had no dollars, so I paid that bill, too.

From Kmart, I took them to a grocery store, where they marveled at the selection of fresh fruit and vegetables. When someone in the group said that this particular grocery store was obviously "only for the elite class in the best neighborhoods," I loaded them into the rental van Tom had arranged for our brief excursion and took them to a grocery store in a rundown inner city Houston neighborhood, where they saw similar inventories. They couldn't believe their eyes. Dr. Sevastianov seemed particularly impressed by what he witnessed.

"They spent $4,000 at Kmart, and marveled at the selection of fresh fruit and vegetables."

Through my continuing studies of the oil situation in the Soviet Union, I learned that Russia's oil production was in a free-fall. Rumor was that production had fallen by 12 percent in 1988 and that it would decline at least another 6 percent the following year.

Because of the money I had already spent hosting the Soviets on their previous trips to Houston — along with my expenses for research and reports I purchased about the Russian oil scene — my accountant told me that he needed to establish a separate company to which he could accrue these costs. I came up with the name VF-Russia. When I established the corporation in 1990, I had serious reservations of doing any business in Russia. I did not have the money for such a venture and I had more than a few reservations about doing business in what was still a Communist country. While I was encouraged by my Soviet colleagues to consider the notion of a joint-venture agreement to drill for oil in the Soviet Union, I had not been formally invited by "official" Russia to consider opening an oil operation there. And I could not imagine receiving an invitation anytime soon.

But that didn't prevent me from doing a little extra homework on my own.

The first investment partners in V-F Russia Inc. were: Bob Berry; Earle Craig, a Midland oil entrepreneur; Jerry; Robert Jenkins, a London-based investment fund manager; and Bill Blakemore, an oil investor from Midland, 1991.

Remote Sensing

I knew the potential for oil production in the Soviet Union was great long before Ward Austin, a gifted scientist and geologist, confirmed my expectations in 1990. I had engaged Ward, an expert in remote sensing, to help me assess the oil potential of the West Siberian Basin in the Soviet Union, if for no other reason than to satisfy my curiosity. And would you believe his amazing work cost just 2 to 4 percent of the expense of traditional seismic evaluations, because, of course, Ward could work remotely using digital imagery from satellites, which is available to US citizens.

By carefully interpreting the images — photos snapped hundreds of miles above the Earth's surface — Ward gauged the size and production potential of prospective oilfields. He specialized in identifying the structural fingerprint of supergiants — a category of underground reservoirs that hold five billion or more barrels of recoverable oil, the mother lode for any oilman.

WHAT LIES BENEATH

Remote sensing is a technique for hydrocarbon and mineral exploration that relies on high-altitude photography and satellite imagery for clues about what lies beneath the ground.

From his home office, Ward would spread out large Mylar films of Mother Earth on a light table and practice his craft — part science, part art — donning a headset affixed with magnifying glasses. Ward would spend hours — often all night long — studying the images from outer space — actually false color composite films overlaid with other high-tech maps. Ward would pencil sketch on an overlain clean sheet of Mylar the landscape features that interested him, features delineating immense underground structures and possible oil

deposits. When he was through, his maps were their own form of art, a rare vista of the world that would fascinate even those uninterested in hydrocarbons.

Over the years, I relied on Ward's work for early reconnaissance. But for the work in Russia, I had planned to use this intelligence for a bit of showmanship.

Jerry in Moscow with Ward Austin, September 25, 1991.

An Exciting Discovery

Ward called me from Sioux Falls, South Dakota, home of the National Satellite Land Remote Sensing Data Archive at the U.S. Geological Survey's Earth Resources Observation and Science (EROS) Center. There, Ward was able to access — anyone may — 40-plus years of satellite remote sensing images free of charge; copies were available for a modest fee.

I had given Ward specific instructions. As he combed through the images of the West Siberian Basin from space — on the lookout for signs of supergiants — he was to focus on prospective targets within a reasonable distance of transport pipelines, all of which were quite visible on the satellite images. The expense to transport oil, especially in remote locations such as Siberia, would be a major factor in any discussion of oil production.

"Do not get more than 50 miles away from a pipeline," I told Ward. "I don't care what you see out there in the boonies of West Siberia. Don't spend any time on it. You stay within 50 miles of a pipeline."

Now, here was Ward, on the phone, sounding like a kid ready to tear into his Christmas gifts.

"Jerry, you won't believe what I'm seeing," he said.

"Is it within 50 miles of a pipe?" I asked.

"Well, no, but let me…"

"No," I interrupted. "I don't want to hear about it. Let's just stay within 50 miles of the pipeline."

"But, Jerry," he said. "I've got to tell you about this."

Asking Ward not to tell you of his latest discovery was difficult, if not impossible. So I relented.

"Jerry, I can't believe what I'm getting ready to tell you. I have found either 19 or 20 supergiant signatures in West Siberia."

"WE'LL SHOW THE RUSSIANS WE'VE DONE A LITTLE HOMEWORK AND SEE WHERE IT GETS US."

"How many of them have been drilled?" I asked, my tone revealing growing interest.

"From what I see… 10 of them, and they all produce, none have been dry holes," he said. "That leaves either nine or 10 undrilled."

He paused a moment.

"Wait, no, there is one more. I've got 11 that are undrilled."

"Holy smokes!" I told Ward, now as enthusiastic as he. "On their next trip over to see us, we'll show the Russians that we've done a little homework. We'll put together a little show and tell and see where it gets us."

Call it hubris or insecurity or another similar factor of motivation, but at my third meeting I wanted to impress the Soviet delegation with my knowledge of the country's oil potential. And Ward's discovery was just the ticket I was looking for.

A Gift

"We've been doing some work, and we found some very interesting things in West Siberia," I began the presentation.

Right off the bat, one of the delegates took the bait and said, "But, you've never been there."

"I know," I replied, with a smile.

"Well, how could you do geologic work in West Siberia? You've never been there."

Without missing a beat, I turned and said, "Let me introduce you to Mr. Ward Austin, a remote sensing expert, and he will explain."

Knowing looks appeared on the faces of two or three of the Soviet oil people. However, most in the room clearly had no clue what remote sensing was. Ward launched into a brief overview of the practice. The moment he concluded, I put on the overhead projector a base image of one of the undrilled supergiant structures in West Siberia that Ward had found during his study of the satellite data.

It didn't take long before the significance of what they were seeing — the site of a supergiant — registered with one of the geologists in the room. He and the few others familiar with remote sensing sat in disbelief of the projected image.

"No, there's nothing like that out there that we haven't found," one man said matter-of-factly. "If there's anything like that in West Siberia, we would have found it and drilled it already."

"Well, this is not drilled," I said, equally as confident as my Russian colleague. "Here's the image. You can see it is not drilled."

"Yes, but you won't tell us where it is. So it is difficult for us to believe this to be true."

"Podarok dlya vashevo buro. Translated to: A gift for your office."

Ward and I were ready. Per our plan of attack on the skeptics, I shot Ward a wink, his signal to place an overlay on top of the base image, showing the surrounding oilfields and their shapes. Supergiants are almost always surrounded by smaller, various-shaped oilfields — fields capable of producing perhaps several hundred million barrels of oil.

The Russians leaned forward in their chairs to take in the new overlay. They started murmuring as they tried to figure out what they were seeing — and the location of the fields.

I winked again. Ward placed a third overlay, this one showing the area's pipelines and railroads. It showed the infrastructure sitting right on top of the supergiant. The Soviets were now fully engaged in the presentation.

"You say this is in West Siberia?" one engineer asked.

"Yes," I replied.

"It looks like it might be near…" another man started to say.

I winked a final time.

Ward placed the last overlay, showing towns and rivers. The room was aghast. Recognizing the location where the Supergiant lie buried, they began frantically filling their notepads like school kids rushing to copy the answer key before the teacher removed it from the blackboard.

"You don't have to write all this down," I told them, delighted by their reaction. "I'm going to give this information to you."

I proceeded to speak my first full sentence in Russian, Podarok dlya vashevo buro. Translated in English, I said: "A gift for your office."

I handed them the maps. "You go drill this, and you'll find it is, indeed, a supergiant."

The Russians were speechless.

Why Me?

For weeks following that third meeting, I didn't know what, if anything, would come of the work that Ward and I presented to the Soviets. I still didn't understand why these top oil people from the Soviet Union found me so interesting and, candidly, why I found them and the Soviet oil challenge equally intriguing.

I had been honest with the Soviets. I pointed out not only their opportunities for potential future success in expanding oil production, but I laid out the serious and expensive problems in their oilfields that needed urgent attention: old, worn-out infrastructure that needed replacement; environmental practices that were scarring the landscape and posing threats to public health and welfare; and corruption — rampant corruption such as open theft of equipment and property from the oilfields.

The whole experience with the Soviets — the dinners, the presentations, the discussions, their seeking my candid advice — was heady stuff for a shrimp-sized independent from West Texas.

"The experience was heady for a small independent oilman from west Texas."

"Soviet bankruptcy was a real possibility."

By this time, early 1991, some of my friends at the Midland Petroleum Club thought I might need mental help. My wife Leah, delighted at first by the sustained enthusiasm the experience provided me, was getting a little weary, if not worried, by my growing interest in the Soviet Union.

I learned later from George Gogonenkov that upon his return from the Houston meetings, he was called in to brief the Deputy Minister of the Oil Ministry. He was in regular contact with Mikhail Gorbachev, general secretary of the Communist Party of the Soviet Union. Gorbachev wanted to reform the Communist system and realized that his only hope for a future without food rationing was to get Russian oil production jump-started quickly. Bankruptcy for the Soviet Union loomed as a real possibility.

Now, Gorbachev wanted the help of Western democracies — our know-how and our money — to turn around the economy of his failing country, following decades of Communist rule and corruption. And, Gorbachev wanted to start in a sector of the Soviet economy where a lifeline existed to a better future — perhaps the only one: oil production.

To accomplish this, Gorbachev needed massive investment from major Western companies to replace aging infrastructure and to expand to new fields — firms like today's ExxonMobil, Chevron, BP and Total — companies whose sizes, orbits and circles I could never touch.

But the majors, at that time, would not give the Soviet oil delegations much help or even advice. Their corporate executives would tell the Russians they have committees looking into the oil potential of Eastern Europe and the Soviet Union and that until their directors gave the green light, they could not be helpful.

Apparently, I was the odd man out — again — because I not only agreed to meet many times with the Soviets, but was willing to offer advice and help to the extent of my limited resources.

All of this was explained to me at our meetings with the delegation of top Russian oil authorities except for one vital factor: why me? Why did the Soviets wish to continue to meet with me? I had some knowledge of the oil business, but I had no experience overseas. I certainly had no big investment money — not the kind needed to help bail out the Soviet Union. Certainly, with all of their intelligence capability, they knew all about me. The question of their obvious interest in me continued in my mind.

George Gogonenkov told me that my decision to meet with the Soviet delegation made a huge impression, if for no other reason than I lived out their fantasy of meeting a Texas independent like they had seen in the movies. To them I was "one of those fabled Texas independent entrepreneurs who knew how to get things done." But more than that, George told me, I had won the personal affection of the Russians — no easy accomplishment since, I learned later, most of them were more skeptical of me than I was of them.

Pushed to tell me how I had earned such trust, George told me, "Jerry, you are the first Westerner in the oil business whom we met that was willing to discuss our problems and get mixed up with us. You gave us ideas and critiques on things that we thought we were going to do, that is until you set us straight. For the first time, they (the Soviets) realized you are not the enemy. You are a real friend, and you are the first one any of us have met."

Mikhail Gorbachev.

"You are the first Western oilman we have met who is willing to be helpful."

— George Gogonenkov

I was amazed by what George said. I acted as I did toward the Soviets because I didn't know any better. I was raised to tell the truth, to live by the Golden Rule and to thank God for his grace and mercy, which I try to do on a daily basis.

I probably didn't realize it fully at the time, but an early sense of my significance to the Soviets came one day when I took a call from an angry Tom Russell in Moscow.

"What the hell are you doing with these Soviets, Jerry?" Tom said. "We've got this mean bastard over here named Vagit Alekperov calling over to the office, wanting to meet you personally in Houston — his assistant asked for you by name — and I know for a fact that this guy is mean, dangerous and can't speak a word of English."

Tom said Alekperov had made the going difficult for their joint venture, MD Seis, by always upping his demands for the Soviet Union.

"He wants to hear you give the presentation you gave the delegation at the last meeting. The oil ministry is abuzz over what you showed them. What's going on with you? If you mess with him (Alekperov), he'll tear you from limb to limb if you're not careful."

I listened until I was certain Tom was finished speaking.

"I'll be careful," I said.

An Invitation to Do Business

The following week, I went to Houston a fourth time to meet another group of Soviet oil authorities at The Houstonian — this one led by Deputy Minister Alekperov, who was one of the youngest deputy ministers in Soviet energy history. I gave the group the same presentation that Ward had helped me prepare, and it was received with similar disbelief and surprise as the first one. The group couldn't believe an American would be so forthcoming with such useful information. And how could anyone know these things, never having set foot in the USSR?

Throughout the presentation, Alekperov sat sober-faced and offered no negative comments or opinions. He was, I learned later, uncharacteristically quiet.

After the meeting, Alekperov called me aside and through his translator began, "This project of yours…" Before he could continue, I was immediately taken aback by his opening statement — project of mine? This certainly wasn't a project that I was going to do — not in my mind.

"This project of yours is of big importance to my country," he said. "When you get to the point that you are willing to pursue this in the field, come see me. I want to help you."

I was stunned by the offer. It was an "official" invitation to work in Russia to explore. It was not any Tom, Dick or Harry who had extended the invitation, it was a personal invitation from the Deputy Minister of the Soviet Ministry of Oil and Gas Industries.

"Any Tom, Dick or Harry had not extended the offer— it was a personal invitation from the Soviet Ministry of Oil and Gas."

And the oilfield I was offered was not a "farm-out" section. It was any oilman's fantasy: a supergiant, capable of producing billions of barrels of oil. Incredible, I thought.

Even a week later, as I tried to force a sense of reality back into my brain, my head spun from the prospect of drilling for oil in Russia. I still thought it was unbelievable!

Twenty-five years earlier, I knew it was a "now or never" deal if I was to start my career as a Texas independent. I took the biggest risk of my life and moved to Midland just as everyone there seemed to be moving out.

Now, at an age that I could begin collecting Social Security, I had been invited to pursue a venture that I knew could instantly absorb all the assets that Leah and I had worked hard to build — and could potentially sink us.

But the opportunity… the more I thought about it, the more I couldn't let it go.

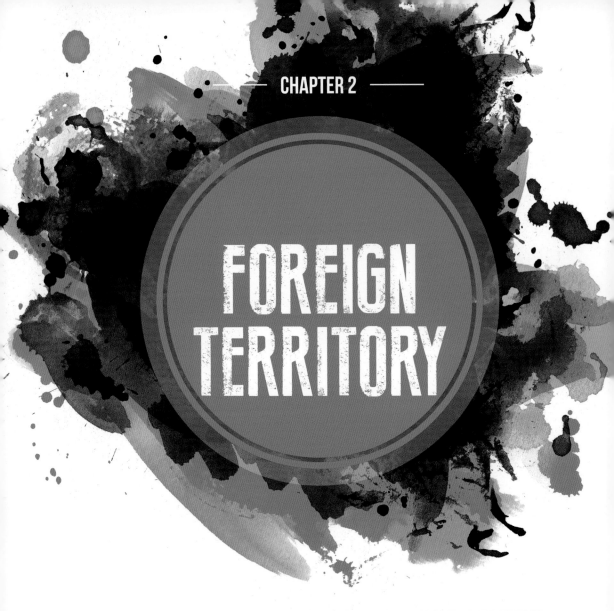

CHAPTER 2

FOREIGN TERRITORY

MAKE NO MISTAKE: THERE WERE LIMITS.

By the spring of 1989 — at about the time that the Soviet oil officials travelled to the U.S. for our initial meeting in Houston — the Soviet Union held its first multi-candidate elections since 1917 to the newly established Congress of People's Deputies. But make no mistake: the openness advocated by *glasnost* (a new way of thinking announced by Gorbachev) had limits. In many Eastern bloc countries and the Soviet Union, secret police routinely repressed — most often through brute force — those who expressed differing views from the ruling Communist party.

"Once tasted, freedom, like toothpaste, cannot be forced back into the tube."

A major turning point in the drama unfolding behind the Iron Curtain came in the summer of 1989 when the Polish people overthrew the Communist government in Warsaw. Soon after, similar uprisings overthrew Communism in the other five Warsaw Pact countries as well.

Gorbachev had lost control of events. To his shock, Gorbachev would later admit, he discovered that the people of Eastern Europe and the Soviet Union did not support his drive to modernize and save Communism. The people wanted to destroy it.

Realizing that he stood little chance at winning any type of foreign investment from Western countries while the Iron Curtain existed, separating East and West — Gorbachev capitulated. He urged orthodox Communist rulers in East Germany, Bulgaria, Czechoslovakia and Romania to enact reforms like those he had advocated for the Soviet Union. Stubborn and misguided, most of them initially refused.

But once tasted, freedom, like toothpaste, cannot easily be forced back into the tube.

The End

Faced with pressure from revolting Soviet republics who took his reforms for openness to heart, Gorbachev made one last-ditch attempt to restructure the Soviet Union into a less centralized state. To accomplish it, he proposed a treaty.

Fifteen days before my first trip to the Soviet Union, a new treaty was scheduled to be signed that would convert the Soviet Union into a federation of independent republics with a common president, foreign policy and military.

"The New Union Treaty" was strongly supported by the Central Asian republics, which needed the economic power and common markets of the other Soviet republics, even though, under treaty terms, it meant the Communist Party would continue to control the economy and social life. But the treaty terms were unacceptable to other reformists who advocated a rapid transition to a market economy — even if it meant the disintegration of the Soviet Union into several independent nation states. Among the supporters of this option was the new President of the Russian Federation Boris Yeltsin. At the opposite extreme, dyed-in-the-wool Communist Party hardliners opposed anything that might contribute to the weakening of the Soviet state and its centralized power base.

On August 19, 1991 — the day before the treaty was to be signed — Gorbachev's vice president, his defense minister, his KGB chief and other senior officials acted to prevent the treaty's signing by forming the "General Committee on State Emergency." The "Committee" placed Gorbachev — on holiday at his *dacha* in Crimea on the Black Sea — under house arrest, reintroduced political and press censorship and attempted to officially end the restructuring policies enacted by Gorbachev.

"From my hotel, I had a clear view of Yeltsin's tanks."

Across the Soviet Union, the reaction was swift and deliberate. The Soviet people responded with a widespread and economically crippling campaign of civil resistance. Thousands of Muscovites surrounded the White House, the name coincidentally given the Russian Federation's parliament, home to Yeltsin's office and the symbolic seat of Russian sovereignty.

Having failed to have Yeltsin arrested, the coup organizers ordered special forces to take up positions near the White House, which by then had been barricaded and protected by Soviet tanks under the control of Yeltsin. After three days, on August 21, the coup collapsed, the organizers were detained and Gorbachev returned as president of the Soviet Union.

On August 24, 1991, reading the proverbial writing on the wall, Gorbachev resigned as General Secretary of the Communist Party of the Soviet Union and ordered all party units in the government dissolved. Five days later, Communist rule in the Soviet Union ended when the Supreme Soviet (the Soviet version of Congress) indefinitely suspended all Communist Party activities on Soviet territory.

I arrived in Moscow a few days later. From my hotel window, I had a good view of the tanks, their ownership now transferred to the Russian Federation and Boris Yeltsin.

Headed to Russia

When I told my friends I was going to Russia to drill for oil, my banker said, "You must be half crazy to go there."

"Yes," I replied, "and I think it helps."

There I was: a lanky, blue-eyed, red-blooded American and devout Presbyterian, a staunch capitalist, and vocally anti-Communist former commissioned officer in the U.S. Navy who served in the Korean and Chinese theaters during the early 1950s. I was headed to the unraveling Soviet Union where Communism had oppressed free enterprise for more than half a century, and where I was considering doing business in the Russian oilfields, home to the largest oil and gas reserves on earth outside of Saudi Arabia.

What was I thinking?

I had been praying since the beginning of this odyssey and while God did not speak to me in a booming voice or a still small voice, I had a sense of calmness and peace about the unfolding developments.

I travelled to the Soviet Union on this first trip with 11 other Americans — experts in their respective oil industry disciplines — who could help me assess what seemed like a once-in-a-lifetime opportunity: to drill for millions of barrels of oil in West Siberia at the invitation of the Soviet government.

"You must be half crazy to go there."

— Jerry's Banker

44

Jerry standing alongside the Moscow River where it passes in front of the Soviet Oil and Gas Ministry (Rossiya Hotel in background), September 23, 1991.

Jerry's first trip to Moscow including meeting with Russian executives at the Transneft offices, September 17, 1991: Ward Austin, Valery Yudin, local geologist, and Jerry.

I had reached out to some professional colleagues, many formerly with DeGolyer and MacNaughton, a premier petroleum consulting firm based in Dallas (with offices in Houston, Moscow, and Calgary). DeGolyer and MacNaughton had been founded in 1936 by oilmen Everette Lee DeGolyer and Lewis MacNaughton — household names when I was growing up.

To finance the trip, I needed $125,000 — money I could not spare. I have been fortunate to know a few men who have invested in my

projects in hopes of receiving a return on their outlay, but not a guaranteed profit. I met with one of these men from Salt Lake City. After explaining the opportunity — and some of the downsides — he agreed to advance the travel funds in exchange for a small interest in any project that may be developed.

I had personally interviewed each of the men who would make the trip with me — a geologist, a petroleum engineer, a reservoir engineer, a drilling engineer, an operations engineer, a remote sensing expert and others whom I

"YOU WILL SEE THINGS NO AMERICAN HAS EVER SEEN."

would rely upon for unbiased advice. I was also fortunate to find an engineer with a business background who spoke Russian, albeit "kitchen Russian," which we needed at that time because only a few Soviets spoke English. Several had arctic drilling and operations experience — all of which was invaluable!

"I cannot afford to pay you your consulting fees if you go on this trip," I told each of the men. But I would pay all expenses, except for liquor and souvenirs. The Soviet oil experts who would be our hosts would take care of our meals and travel while we were on the three-week adventure.

"You will see things no American has ever seen — it will be an experience you will remember the rest of your lives," I said. Despite no formal compensation, each man immediately accepted the invitation.

A Glimpse at Dim Russia

We arrived on September 4, 1991, at Sheremetyevo-2 Airport in Moscow, where we were greeted not by the welcome wagon, but soldiers with guns who ordered us to line up for inspection and approval from Customs. Ogled with evil eyes — Americans were still the enemy in those days — we were canvassed up and down and peppered with questions about our luggage. Finally, we were cleared and sent on our way to the main airport lobby where we encountered a crush of people.

"Taxi? Taxi? Taxi?"

The chorus from hungry taxi drivers echoed loudly throughout the lobby. We had arranged private transport to our downtown Moscow hotel, an hour away — there were too many newspaper stories of foreigners taking Moscow cabs and disappearing until a hefty ransom had been paid.

As we entered downtown Moscow, I noticed that the streets were empty and the storefronts were dark, even though the weather was pleasant — cool, but not cold. I soon discovered why. There were almost no restaurants, no pubs, no convenience stores, and no fast-food joints; there was nowhere to go, nothing to do. Nobody was on the streets.

Moscow was dark and it was not due solely to the setting September sun. The place itself was unlit; And the darkness, dramatic and foreboding, seemed to reflect the mood of the people: dark. I wasn't shocked by the gloomy nature of Moscow on my first visit to the Soviet Union — the place had suffered under Communist rule for more than 70 years, after all — but I was surprised by the dullness of the Russian capital.

"There were stories of foreigners disappearing."

The next morning, I arose for my daily walk of a mile or two. Although the sun shone brightly, few people were on the street and those whom I passed by would make no eye contact with me, let alone offer a stranger a friendly smile.

The daylight revealed dirty and dusty storefront windows that, oddly, had no signs telling would-be shoppers what they offered for sale. Peering through some of the shop windows, I noticed an interesting pattern: faded crepe paper, once fresh and colorful, had been styled as makeshift curtains around window displays; the paper curtains were dark red, deep orange, black or gray — the official colors of Soviet commerce, I wondered?

I ventured into a few shops to see what I might buy for Leah or others back home. My Russian, restricted then to a few greetings memorized from guidebooks, proved fruitless: the stores had nothing for sale. Literally, they had no inventory. I knew from my reading that the Soviet economy was in shambles with runaway inflation. (In 1991, the ruble traded at 100 to the U.S. dollar; by 1993, it would trade at 1,024 to the dollar as inflation hovered at about 20 percent a month. The average Russian wage then was about 23,000 rubles a month).

I wasn't shocked by what I saw in the Moscow stores, or didn't see — the result of decades of market oppression, restriction and control — but I was surprised at how I felt about the situation: heartsick for the Soviet people. No wonder shopping at the Houston Kmart had captivated the Soviets whom I had hosted on one of their earlier trips to the U.S. The comparison was shocking.

Semi-Darkness

At a meeting later that day, I got a first-hand experience of the quality of life in the Soviet Union, circa 1991. Dr. George Gogonenkov, the Russian oil official whom I now considered a friend, had invited our group to a large conference room in the Central Geophysical Expedition (CGE) building to begin reviewing maps of prospective oilfields in West Siberia.

Sunlight from large bay windows flooded the conference room, and was the only source of light. As the maps were rolled out, I asked George if he could turn the room lights on. He did so, cheerfully. The moment he discerned that the lights were no longer needed, he turned them off. If needed again, the lights went on — and then off.

"George, why don't you leave the lights on? Is the electricity so expensive?" I asked.

"No," he replied. "It's practically free. But if we burn out the bulbs, we could not get any replacements, so we don't turn the lights on."

This was the practice all over the Soviet Union: one navigates life in semi-darkness because the bulbs might burn out. This was the custom in homes, offices, churches and while driving vehicles.

It was as if the bulbs were being saved for something. But what? The logic escaped me.

"It was as if the bulbs were being saved."

Our crew gathered around Nikolai Lisovsky, chairman of the Central Development Commission of Hydrocarbon Fields in Russia, looking at a large map.

Jerry in the general director's office at the Orenburgneft headquarters in Orenburg, September 9, 199

Assessing the Oil Situation

The overview of the oil situation in the Soviet Union took up the first two days of our stay in Moscow and confirmed what I already knew: the Soviet oil industry would require decades to restore, rehabilitate and reform. Not only was the broken and aging oil infrastructure in need of physical repair and replacement, but the management of the state-run oil companies was deeply dysfunctional and rumored to be corrupt.

I took comfort in knowing that George Gogonenkov and the other Soviet officials we met with — good oil people, all knowledgeable and passionate about the business — agreed with most of my appraisal of the situation. I supported their position that the best solution would lie in Western-style management reforms, best implemented by opening the Soviet Union's vast oil reserves to foreign know-how, innovation and investment.

It did not escape me that a small-fry outfit from Midland, Texas, was now in high-level meetings with the Soviet Union's top oil officials — at a time when the country was amidst a political transformation of historic dimensions. Not only was I a witness to history, I was, in a small way, a participant in making a bit of it.

It was a huge opportunity — I could become the first independent oil operator in history to successfully drill, recover and sell oil from the Soviet Union — and that certainly weighed on my mind. While I saw this chance as an opportunity to make some good money, I was equally driven by the thrill of the pursuit — the planning, preparation and execution phases — to reach pay zones in a part of the world that most oil men only dreamed about.

No Thank You

To help our team assess the project and to better understand the big picture of oil operations in the Soviet Union, our Soviet hosts had scheduled a series of meetings. We journeyed on planes, trains, automobiles and buses across the vast Soviet Union.

I was most excited by the helicopter ride to the Russkaya field in West Siberia, about 2,000 miles northeast of Moscow, where I had been invited to explore production possibilities.

This adventure was why I had spent a small fortune — and now nearly two years of my life — to bring the team of oil experts to the Soviet Union. I was eager to see up close the oilfields in West Siberia, one of which, Vagit Alekperov, the Soviet Union's Deputy Oil Minister, had personally invited me to seriously consider.

The deal terms were excellent. My company, VF-Russia, would front all the production costs and keep 100 percent of revenues (and pay no taxes) until we had recovered our capital investment and expenses. Then, we would split resulting revenues 50-50 for the life of the project.

The Russkaya field was vast, with an estimated yield of eight-and-one-half billion barrels of recoverable oil. The project would generate hundreds of billions of dollars during its production cycle. The Soviets had already spent nearly $1 billion proving the field's potential by drilling some 340 test wells — but, inexplicably, had developed none of them into producing wells.

"The challenges were immense, but I still wanted to see the end of the Earth."

As I was told, all of these wells were "geological wells" — not "production wells." When I observed the number of geological wells drilled and huge funds expended with no thought of converting the field into a paying proposition, it became obvious to me that this was at least one example of why the Soviet oil industry was in such trouble.

But the challenges posed by working in such remote fields were immense. First, most of the well work would have to be done during winter — when the ground was frozen and vehicles could reach the site; infrastructure — roads, tanks, pipeline, housing, office space — would have to be engineered and constructed; and logistics — regular deliveries of needed supplies, materials and people — would require a Herculean effort and huge investment of funds, quite beyond the capabilities of any small company, and especially mine.

Knowing all of this, I still wanted to see the place — and that required a helicopter ride, a long helicopter ride — to the end of the Earth, or not far from the northern end, anyway.

"Take me back, I'm not interested in this project."

In West Siberia, towns are built from scratch. Settlers chop down trees, clear space and build their towns. The prevailing architecture is plain and simple concrete block structures, left in their natural gray or painted muted beige. They are built close to one another, and although they look alike, the buildings carry no signs. Signs don't last the harsh winters, when temperatures regularly drop to 30 to 40 degrees below zero.

From the window of our lumbering Soviet helicopter — a large military issue that could carry up to 20 passengers — I could see the towns, which became fewer and fewer as we flew hundreds of miles to our destination, the Russkaya oilfield. Soon, there were no towns to see, no roads, no electrical lines, no pipelines — all left some 60 to 80 miles behind us. Below, lakes and ponds, a few large ones, pocked the surface like bad acne, and much of the land was swampy; there were very few trees, and what trees there were, stood clumped in small groups like tiny islands.

After hours of travel, we finally arrived at the oilfield. After circling for what seemed like an eternity, our pilot finally spotted a decent-sized patch of dry land to put the helicopter down. I got out, took a deep breath and told our Russian hosts, "Take me back to the house. I'm not interested in this project."

They were incredulous. Through an interpreter, one mid-level bureaucrat said, "There are eight-and-a-half billion barrels of oil right where you are standing!"

Perhaps that was so. But standing in the middle of only God knew where — literally, we were hundreds of miles from the nearest town — I

Getting ready to board a helicopter for a trip to view oil fields in the West Siberian wilderness, September 12, 1991.

calmly explained my disinterest and reminded my hosts of the mini-lecture that I had given them in Houston.

"The really big payoff for the entrepreneur is to see his project, his baby, come alive and be born," I told them. "If he's an architect, he wants to see the building built. If he's an artist, he wants to see his painting finished and hanging in a museum. If he's an oilman, he wants to see the field developed and producing oil."

"You're not going to have electricity out here for 25 years — even if you started tomorrow," I said. "I'm 62 years old, you do the math. Now take me to the house. I'm not interested."

Pick of the Litter

After the long helicopter ride back to Langepas, an oil town of 41,000 residents, about 1,400 miles northeast of Moscow, our group gathered in a conference room of the local state-owned oil company, Langepasneftegaz. The Soviet oil official who just hours before had been dumbfounded by my rejection of the oil-rich Russkaya field asked a question through his interpreter that he must have been mulling on the long trip back.

"What do you want, anyway?" he asked. "We want you over here doing business. What would you like to have?"

A large map of the Soviet Union — probably 20 feet wide by 10 feet high — occupied a conference room wall. Walking over to it, I pointed to an area in Southern Russia, just north of the Russian border with Kazakhstan, near the Caspian Sea — a proven area of oil and gas production called the Volga-Ural region, so named for the Volga River and the Ural Mountains.

"I would like to get a project in this area to develop and work on," I said. From my research, I knew this to be an independent oil operator's heaven — an area holding five or six different oil pay zones, all above 5,000 feet, much shallower than the fields of West Siberia, where a driller would have to go to 9,000 to 11,000 feet down to reach only two pay zones.

Pointing to the map, I said: "You've got rivers over here with barges, you've got trains, highways, pipelines, electricity; you've got everything already built out. If I find a promising field, I can get electricity easily, pipelines are available and the roads I can use."

A geophysical analyst, Nikolai Lisovsky (the most important oil official in the Soviet Union), Jerry, and George Gogonenkov, September 23, 1991.

A look of alarm came over the face of the Soviet oil official. "No, you cannot get in there," he replied quickly. "That area is closed. No Westerners are allowed."

I was ready with a reply of my own.

"Then you tell (Soviet Oil) Minister (Leonid) Filimonov, if he wants independent oil producers to come to Russia, this is the kind of area in which they would want to be active," I said. "Based on what you're saying to me, I'm not sure he really wants us in Russia. I can see all kinds of problems we'd have to deal with anyway. But, if he is serious about wanting us over here, he needs to open up areas like this."

The Soviet oil official said, "There's no way we can do that."

Wait and See

The collapse of the Soviet Union, the last unifying force in the country, came swiftly throughout the fall and early winter of 1991. Ten republics declared their independence between August and December, and eventually Russia, by now under Yeltsin, moved to take over the remaining assets of the Soviet government, now the Russian government, including the Kremlin.

In a two-year period, 1990 to 1992, the former Soviet Union had lost one third of its territory, which had been home to half of its population. Much of the land had been under central rule since 1700. By any measure, the revolution was historic. Watching it unfold from the sidelines — heck, being in the middle in the earliest days of independent Russia — was unbelievable.

But many questions begged answers. Would the lights finally come on in Russia? Would the dark place that Moscow had become ever brighten?

As for me, I was truly headed to the house — my home, back in Midland. On September 25, 1991, our entourage left Moscow for the long flight to Texas. Our trip had been exciting and illuminating — but somewhat frustrating.

For me, Russia had become a game — of wait and see — or maybe, forget it.

"Russia had become a game— of wait and see— or maybe, forget it."

CHAPTER 3

WE'RE IN BUSINESS

A CABLE ARRIVED FROM MOSCOW.

In November 1991, six weeks after my return to the United States, a cable from Moscow arrived at my Midland office. The message underscored what I had been told by George Gogonenkov, early on in our acquaintance: "In Russia, nothing is ever as it appears."

"I was enthralled at the prospect of living on the front row of history."

The cable, addressed to me personally, announced that Leonid Filimonov, at that time the Soviet minister of oil and gas industries, had opened five additional areas for oil development that had been previously closed to Western oil companies. Among the newly accessible areas was a relatively small patch in the Volga Ural Basin, which had looked promising during my September trip to the Soviet Union, at least on paper. I was not surprised by the news from Minister Filimonov, but I was pleased because the Russians had listened to me. They knew I was right and that only by opening prospective areas where infrastructure was already in place would they attract the interest and investment that was badly needed from independent oil operators.

As I made plans to return to Moscow to explore these opportunities first hand, I could only imagine what chaos I would find politically. The experience was surreal — and I was enthralled at the prospect of living it from history's front row.

The Former Soviet Union

By December 21, 1991, all of the republics (except for Georgia, which didn't feel it was necessary) had signed an agreement to dissolve the Soviet Union.

On December 24, the Soviet Ambassador to the United Nations informed the U.N. that Russia was to be the successor state to the Soviet Union for purposes of U.N. membership. The other 14 independent states established from the former Soviet Republics were all eventually admitted to the U.N. as sovereign nations.

On December 25, Gorbachev (who had accepted the dissolution of the Soviet Union a week earlier at a meeting with Yeltsin) resigned as president of the Union of Soviet Socialist Republics, declaring the office extinct and yielding all control to the Russian president. That night, the Soviet flag was lowered over the Kremlin for the last time.

By December 31, the few Soviet institutions that hadn't been taken over by Russia had terminated operations, as individual republics assumed the role of the former central government. Needless to say, the immensely valuable Ministry of Oil and Gas was among the first assets seized by Russia.

"By December they had dissolved the Soviet Union."

Yeltsin Takes Control

In January 1992, the former U.S.S.R. was in chaos. Overnight, what had been one country had been split into 15 separate republics. The Russian Federation, led by President Boris Yeltsin, would determine the way forward for nearly 300 million people living in what had been the world's largest state, a vast area spread across 11 time zones (now nine).

Yeltsin had no plan for the new Russia. Surprised by his quick ascent to power, the former construction site foreman flew by the seat of his pants. He understood that Westernizing Russia's depressed and stagnant economy and attracting huge foreign investment was the only way to stimulate even an adequate way forward.

But with shards of Communism deeply embedded in the government of the former Soviet Union, ridding Russia of party hardliners proved an arduous task. By early 1992, with inflation and general lawlessness spiraling out of control, the Russian people were on the verge of panic.

From my early experience with the Soviet Union, I referred to the businessmen I encountered as Soviets or comrades. But, as Yeltsin took over and the Soviet Union dissolved, I began referring to my colleagues as Russians. Certainly, the ethnic background of the population was more than just Russian but, the Russian people are proud to be Russian and throughout my time there I strived to always show them and their culture the proper respect.

Returning to Russia

Such was the political backdrop when I flew into Moscow on January 18, 1992 — the 24th day of the new Russia — where George Gogonenkov, my "Russian Godfather," met me at the airport. Jokingly, I still refer to George as my "Russian Godfather" not because of any nefarious activities on his part — there were none — but because he continued to oversee my comings and goings without any remuneration. Not only was George well connected — he remained First Deputy Director of the Central Geophysical Expedition, which provided seismic studies and other oil exploration services across Russia, — but he was (and is to this day) a true gentleman. His advice, knowledge and sensibilities would become invaluable to me in the years to come.

After a day of preparatory meetings, George and I took a two-hour flight to the ancient Russian city of Orenburg, about 900 miles southeast of Moscow. Located on the banks of the Ural River and close to the border of neighboring Kazakhstan, Orenburg is the administrative center of the Orenburgskaya Oblast (region). It was established in 1743 by Russian diplomat and administrator Ivan Ivanovich Neplyuyev, who had a prominent position in the service of Peter the Great and Catherine the Great. Orenburg served as a vital military outpost in its early history, and became home to the Orenburg Cossacks who protected the land from the nomadic Kazakhs while it was being colonized.

"My 'Russian Godfather' was invaluable to me."

A field development meeting in Orenburg with the BaiTex chief engineer and chief electrician.

The purpose of our trip to Orenburg was to meet with officials from the Russian oil company Orenburgneft (*neft* is the Russian word for oil) (OBN), which, in those days, was still owned by the Russian government, but would soon be absorbed by the giant Tyumen Oil Company of western Siberia. The company was known by its Russian acronym "TNK," and was one of the country's largest and newest privately owned enterprises.

In a conference room at the headquarters of OBN, we met with company geologists and engineers who had laid out maps of the five areas now open to Westerners for drilling. Although other potential foreign investors would have opportunities to pursue oil deals in Russia, newly established relationships with Russian oil officials in Moscow helped me get in early, which is key for any independent oil operator who wants to be successful anywhere in the world.

The Baituganskoye Field

I was focused on potential opportunities in the Volga Ural Oil Basin, a well-known oil region in Russia where drilling had first begun in late 1920. The necessary infrastructure — roads, electricity, pipelines and housing — was already in place, and most importantly the region's oilfields had numerous proven oil pay zones, shallow and deep.

I had zeroed in on an oily patch known as the Baituganskoye field. It was situated about 90 miles northwest of Orenburg and was isolated from other, larger oilfields that I had hoped would be open for exploration and drilling.

During my September trip to Russia, I had figured that the Baituganskoye field was a "one-off" field that OBN might be eager to unload to a foreign investor — a guy like me.

The topographic map that George and I had studied in our prep meetings showed grain patterns of the substructure beneath the Baituganskoye field, a nice size at about 12,500 acres. One-third of the field had been already drilled before the wells were abandoned for "richer drilling" elsewhere, or so it was explained to us.

Novousmanova, the nearest town to the Baituganskoye field, in Russia's Volga-Ural region.

I couldn't imagine a more promising site for oil than the Baituganskoye field; Test wells had conclusively shown oil in huge shallow reservoirs 3,000 to 3,500 feet below ground. At that time, a well could be put in operation for $30,000 each, compared to $400,000 to $500,000 today. The cinch came when one of the engineers revealed that the site had a pipeline pump station that would ship oil directly into Transneft — the state-controlled national oil pipeline system, the largest in the world. No oil trucks would be required to carry crude, a security risk, sadly, because of the widely accepted practice of drivers skimming oil during their runs.

"Let's go up and look at the field and meet the people there," I said to the OBN folks.

The mosque at Novousmanova.

Love at First Sight

The Baituganskoye field was a three-hour drive north and west of Orenburg, and was located on a hill that had been created by faults between which pooled an estimated 110 million barrels of recoverable oil. For me, it was love at first sight.

The field itself was littered with old equipment, contaminated pockets of oily soil and was generally unkempt. But even before we ever began our tour of the site, I had already pictured the place in my mind's eye — after a thorough cleaning, it would be a beautiful oilfield, surrounded as it was in a gorgeous setting of rolling hills blanketed by virgin forests, which permeated the air with a fresh odor.

At the foot of the hill sat Novousmanova, a little town of about 400 people. Goats and chickens grazed in the backyards of the small homes in the town, which existed solely because of the Baituganskoye field. Not far away was the city of Buguruslan, founded in 1748, that was home to about 50,000 residents.

The Baituganskoye oilfield before BaiTex cleaned them up and restarted operations.

A typical Russian village.

The people of Novousmanova greeted us warmly; the women had fixed us a huge lunch of lamb, sausage and fresh vegetables — all homegrown ingredients. On a town walkthrough, I quickly became impressed by the inventiveness of the mostly poor population. The town had a community tool shed, for example, where the men made whatever they needed — whether gears for a vehicle or parts for a broken washing machine.

If we ever needed a part or a repair for a well, I imagined that these Russians could make it or fix it — another positive indicator that I added to my growing list of pros supporting a potential oil deal there. Because the oilfield had not been in full production for several years, the townspeople told me through translators that they were eager for more work.

Excited to Make the Deal

Trying to restrain my excitement, I asked one of the top engineers from OBN who accompanied us on the trip why the company chose not to more heavily fish in what clearly appeared to me a well-stocked pond.

The engineer explained that Rem Khramov, the powerful General Director of OBN, wanted to pull the company's presence and investment from the field because it was "too small" and "off by itself," making its operations less efficient — a rationale I had anticipated.

In short, the engineer said, there were bigger fish for OBN to catch in larger, well-stocked ponds. (Russia's second largest oilfield, for example, the Romashkino field — discovered in 1948 — is the largest oilfield of the Volga-Ural Basin and sits 400 miles north of Orenburg.)

OBN was eager to find a prospective partner to take over the Baituganskoye field, the engineer said, ridding the company of a one-off (while also keeping the partner away from the larger fields, I figured). The Baituganskoye field was ripe for a joint venture — a joint venture between an American oil company and an emerging free-market oil company in Russia, OBN.

If the deal terms would be roughly the same as they were for the Russkaya field in west Siberia and OBN would agree to transfer the oil license to the new company that I would establish to operate the joint venture, we had a deal.

Returning to Orenburg, I told the OBN officials that I wanted to make a deal; we needed to put together a written agreement, and without hesitation, the OBN management team agreed to move forward.

Because nothing like it had existed before in the history of Russia, the contract between OBN and the new company I called "BaiTex" took months to prepare. The company name

"Without hesitation they agreed to move forward on a deal."

combined the location of my new venture and my home — "Bai" was shorthand for the Baituganskoye field and "Tex," of course, referred to Texas, home to seven generations of my family.

Under the proposed terms, BaiTex would front all the production costs and keep 100 percent of revenues (and pay no taxes) until we had recovered our capital investment and expenses. Then, BaiTex and OBN would split resulting revenues 50-50 for the life of the project. Most importantly, OBN would transfer the license to the field required by the Russian government, thus allowing BaiTex to sell oil into the market.

"DON'T MAKE ANY PAYOFFS AND DON'T ACCEPT ANY PAYOFFS."

— DON ZARIN

Help From Home

Back in Moscow, I huddled with our U.S.-based lawyers to hammer out a proposed joint venture agreement. As we prepared to start our work, I arranged a meeting in Moscow with a trade representative at the United States Embassy. If the U.S. government had any concerns about my doing a deal in Russia, I wanted to know about it now. I was relieved to learn my government wanted U.S. oil deals in Russia.

The trade official said, "We see your efforts as part of a huge opportunity to create new sources of oil in Russia that can wean us off the Middle East. Your plan is exactly our plan, so go ahead and do what you can do."

Because I had no international business experience, I also hired a well-known Washington attorney with experience in Russia to advise me on the ins-and-outs of doing business there. His initial counsel caught me off guard.

"Don't make any payoffs and don't accept any payoffs," Don Zarin told me, sounding like the expert he is. Author of *Doing Business Under the Foreign Corrupt Practices Act*, Don literally wrote the textbook on anti-corruption practices overseas. I assured Don that payoffs of any kind in Russia wouldn't be an issue. Not only did I have no money to offer bribes, my Presbyterian roots certainly would not permit me to accept any. I just did not know how to play that game.

Getting Serious, Setting Up Shop

With preparation of a formal agreement under way, I moved quickly to line up initial project investors to purchase equipment, hire personnel and establish offices; I would show the Russians that I was serious about doing business.

Through phone calls, I secured about $400,000 from two longtime friends; I secured another $5 million investment from the British Framlington Russian Investment Fund, overseen by its chairman, The Right Honorable Geoffrey Howe, who previously served as Margaret Thatcher's deputy prime minister; and, Leah and I were prepared to fund what we could from our resources to get the operation started.

In the spring of 1992 with the BaiTex negotiations underway, I knew I would be returning to Moscow on a regular basis; I also realized that I could no longer afford to spend $325 a night for a hotel room in downtown Moscow. I needed an apartment and an office in Moscow. George Gogonenkov took care of the latter, setting me up temporarily in a small office closet in the building where he worked, and helping me recruit personnel, starting with an English-speaking administrative assistant, Natasha Malakova, whom I hired for $100 per month to help me establish my Russian operation (a great salary at the time by Russian standards). We stayed in the temporary office for a few years until our operation grew and required more personnel and space.

George assigned the task of finding me an apartment to one of his administrative assistants — a no-nonsense, multi-talented woman named Nadyezda Koslova whom everyone called Nadia. Nadia soon found a suitable two-bedroom apartment with a living room, kitchen

Jerry and Orenburgneft senior staff members discuss the project Jerry is about to undertake in Russia. The woman translating for Jerry is his first Russian employee, Natasha Malakova.

Buguruslan, where BaiTex's administrative offices were located, September 19, 1991.

and single bathroom that rented for $400 per month and was just two blocks away from the office. I grabbed it, and with Leah's help, I promptly went to work remodeling it. Eventually as rent began to climb due to inflation and our landlord needed the apartment, we moved to a larger apartment in Moscow.

On my first trip to Russia, Gogonenkov also introduced me to Valery Yudin, an impressive Russian oil executive, who served as a wonderful resource for me. When I later needed someone to manage the BaiTex operation, I hired Yudin, who is a Russian Jew and a very smart, earnest and hardworking man with a great understanding of Russian history and culture. He holds degrees in math,

physics, and geophysics, including a doctorate. Throughout my time in Russia, Yudin proved to be an invaluable asset to me and the BaiTex operation.

When we later moved from Gogonenkov's offices, we rented office space in Moscow until a few years later when the building owner told us we would need to relocate as the building was for sale and we would no longer be able to rent. With Moscow office rents soaring — some American firms paid up to $30,000 a month for downtown office space — we were forced to buy as there was nothing available to rent. We ended up purchasing an office building two blocks from Gogonenkov at the CGE building in a safe neighborhood outside downtown.

Invitation to the White House

At the time, I did not realize what a big deal — at least symbolically — that other Russians considered our pending BaiTex deal with OBN. I would discover how significant in September 1993, when I was invited to the White House to meet with Vice President Al Gore and Russian Prime Minister Viktor Chernomyrdin.

The two leaders co-chaired the Gore-Chernomyrdin Commission, the first-of-its-kind initiative between the United States and Russia that U.S. President Bill Clinton and Russian President Yeltsin had agreed to establish during a special summit in Vancouver in April 1993. The purpose of the commission was to increase co-operation between the two countries in the areas of energy, space exploration, trade and business, science and technology, agribusiness and defense conversion.

I was invited to attend the commission's first meeting on energy, which was held in the Treaty Room of the White House. Russia, after all, was — and remains — an energy superpower, possessing the world's largest natural gas reserves, the second largest coal reserve, and producing more barrels of crude oil than any country except Saudi Arabia.

Taking My Place at the Head Table

Arriving at the White House a half-hour ahead of the meeting, I was escorted to the Treaty Room, which was smaller than I had anticipated. As I was early, I began looking at the name plates on the various chairs set up in the room in front of the conference table where the big-wigs would speak. I couldn't find my name on a chair so I asked a White House page to bring one for me.

While waiting for the page to return, my curiosity got the best of me, and I began reading the nameplates of those who would sit at the head table. I saw where Vice President Gore and Prime Minister Chernomyrdin would sit, as well as Energy Secretary Hazel O'Leary, Undersecretary of State Nicholas Burns and other American and Russian dignitaries. Interspersed among the officials I saw nameplates for the chairmen or presidents of Goldman Sachs, Boeing, Texaco and Chevron. And then, to my enormous surprise, I saw my name: Jerome Fullinwider, President of VF-Russia. I was seated at the head table!

(A few months later, I learned how I was placed there. A high-ranking Russian official named Nikolai Lisovsky, Chairman of the Central Development Commission of Hydrocarbon Fields, and who would later lead the Ministry of Fuel and Energy, had forwarded my name to the U.S. State Department as the Russian government's official nominee to attend the energy panel.)

"If some shady deals were made, it would be a small price to pay."

As official host for the meeting, Vice President Gore asked each of us to introduce ourselves. When it was my turn, I said: "When the President of Texaco is introduced, the world applauds, and no further information is necessary. But when I introduce myself as President of VF-Russia, perhaps some explanation is necessary." The crowd erupted in laughter, breaking the stilted atmosphere.

When my turn came to speak — my remarks were unprepared, unlike those of my panel colleagues — I spoke of changes needed in Soviet legislation to even the playing field for independent oil operators who were competing against the Texacos of the world. I concluded by discussing a subject none of the U.S. majors would touch: the incompetence of Russian oil executives and managers, ineptitude bred by decades of state-owned control.

"If Russia really wanted its oil managers to learn how to negotiate and trade in the international way, the quickest and best way to do this is not to send them to Harvard or Wharton, but to cut them loose to deal directly with their Western counterparts," I told the crowd. "They would learn overnight! And if some shady deals were made, that would be a small price for Russia to pay to educate its corps of oil managers."

I told the truth.

Meeting the Energy Secretary

After the meeting ended, Mrs. O'Leary, the most improbable Energy Secretary that God ever knew, approached me. "Mr. Fullinwider, I enjoyed what you had to say so much," she said, holding out her hand and introducing herself. "I don't know anything about the oil business."

I said, "That's very refreshing to hear, Hazel, because I assume you don't and most officials in your position would not admit to that."

"Well, I readily admit to it. You have some experience where most of us haven't. Could I call you and talk to you about problems as they come up and could you meet me here in my office if I need you?"

"Of course," I replied, giving her a card. I never heard from Hazel O'Leary. I did, however, subsequently meet with Undersecretary of State Nicholas Burns at his request; he is an erudite and fascinating man who cares deeply for the nation's welfare.

Pioneer Priority Project

A few months after the meeting in Washington, I received some good news — the result of my five minutes of White House fame. The Gore-Chernomyrdin Commission named the BaiTex Project, one of only five "Pioneer Priority Projects" named by the joint U.S.-Russian initiative. The designation floored me as the other four projects were multi-billion dollar ventures involving major Western companies.

The projects selected as Pioneer Priority Projects were projects that both the American and Russian governments particularly wanted to see succeed. Both governments committed to watching over these protected projects. A Russian friend had submitted our name for consideration, as he wanted to see a small operation make it in Russia. He also realized the other four Pioneer Priority Projects were huge and would take years to work out, while mine was much smaller and would take much less time. Once my deal was worked through, they could use my story to encourage others to engage in business in Russia.

I later learned the Pioneer Priority Projects were never announced publicly, so it was never fully known that the governments were backing each project. Being a Pioneer Priority Project proved to be valuable leverage for me later, however, as I struggled to keep afloat in Russia.

Negotiating the BaiTex Deal

Throughout the negotiation process, I tried to earn the favor of Rem Khramov, the powerful and crusty General Director of OBN. General Directors of the state-owned oil companies were big authority figures in Russia, akin to 1950s union bosses in the United States. Frankly, I don't think Khramov took our deal seriously — largely because I was not like any oilman he knew. The oilmen he knew did not wear suits, speak intelligently, ask questions out of intellectual curiosity or discuss their artistic interests.

I tried to crack the stern façade of the chain-smoking oil executive by bringing him cartons of Marlboro cigarettes — highly sought overseas treasure — as a gesture of friendship. An American friend once chided me for doing so.

"Jerry, you don't smoke and you don't allow smoking in your office," my friend said. "Why do you give American cigarettes to Khramov?"

I replied, "If you have smelled the Russian cigarettes, you'd realize I am trying to clean up the atmosphere."

Khramov did not negotiate the details of our contract because our deal was small potatoes for OBN, involving only the remaining 80 million barrels of oil — not the billion-plus barrel deals that Khramov sought. In West Texas, an 80 million barrel deal in 1992 would have been front-page news in the Midland Reporter-Telegram. In Russia, world giants like British Petroleum and Exxon were getting the press attention on new billion-dollar deals.

Our agreement details were left to the OBN chief geologist, Peter Postojenko, to negotiate. A bright and personable fellow, Peter was nothing if not thorough. He read every word of our proposed agreement multiple times and asked for the precise meaning of about every fifth word. He knew — we knew — that if one "i" wasn't dotted or one "t" wasn't crossed, Khramov would delay, if not axe the deal. Because documents were prepared and then revised in both Russian and English literally dozens of times, the negotiations sputtered along at a snail's pace.

Finally...A Signed Deal

In early September 1993 — after 18 months of painstaking negotiations between BaiTex and OBN — we concluded an agreement that Peter Postojenko said he would recommend General Director Khramov sign. Under the terms, BaiTex provided capital, equipment, technology and management to oversee and retrain the oilfield workers in the Baituganskoye field. BaiTex would deliver the oil, OBN would sell it, and both firms would share the profits equally after OBN reimbursed BaiTex the initial investment and operating costs and transferred the oilfield license to BaiTex.

With George Gogonenkov's assistance, we scheduled a signing ceremony of two contracts — one in Russian, one in English — in the large conference room of the former Soviet Oil Ministry Building in Moscow on September 15, 1993.

The agreement with Orenburgneft is finally signed.

The team that signed the original contract between Orenburgneft and VF-Russia: George Gogonenkov, first deputy director of the Central Geophysical Expedition in Moscow; Jerry; Rem Khramov, Peter Postojenko, OBN chief geologist, September 15, 1993.

"NYET.
I HAVE OTHER PLANS."

— GENERAL DIRECTOR REM KHRAMOV

For most of us present, the moment was clearly historic. The agreement represented the first joint venture deal between an American independent oil company and a Russian-owned oil company. I was elated at the signing ceremony, but Mr. Khramov clearly was not.

Even at the final moment, it didn't appear Khramov believed in — or necessarily wanted to be bothered by — the deal. As he leaned forward to sign the contract, he hesitated a moment. Speaking in his native Russian, he said, according to my Russian friends, "Well, I guess we'll go ahead and sign this thing. I never thought it would come to this." And he signed it.

After a few photographs to capture the occasion, I invited Khramov, through his translator, to join us for a celebratory dinner — my treat.

"Nyet," the General Director replied, "I have other plans."

The sign at BaiTex's Baituganskoye field announcing the road going into Novousmanova.

Well testing at No. 128, the first BaiTex production oil well.

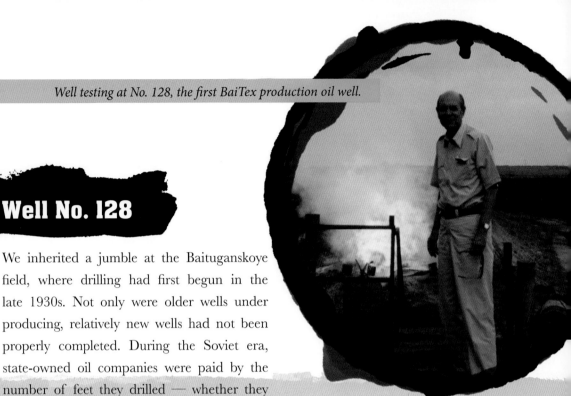

Well testing at No. 128, the first BaiTex production oil well.

Well No. 128

We inherited a jumble at the Baituganskoye field, where drilling had first begun in the late 1930s. Not only were older wells under producing, relatively new wells had not been properly completed. During the Soviet era, state-owned oil companies were paid by the number of feet they drilled — whether they struck oil or not.

The field itself was a mess. The Soviets cared not a penny about the environmental desolation their haphazard operations created, witness the dead trees, lakes of oil, dead fish and animals and old rusty heaps covering the moon-like

The first well, No. 128, brought online by BaiTex.

A field office building in Novousmanova, the nearest village to the Baituganskoye field.

landscape. Under Soviet Socialism, no one owns anything, so there's no pride in keeping up property. Not surprisingly, this type of grim Socialism is linked to the world's worst polluters.

Through our efforts, BaiTex earned the loyalty of the townspeople of Novousmanova. We started by cleaning up the Baituganskoye field. Eventually, I hired 96 full-time employees in the field and in Buguruslan, the small city where we had an administrative office. We also had another 11 employees in Moscow.

One day, completely out of left field, a scrap dealer showed up at the field and offered to haul away the huge piles we had collected — and he said he would pay us to do so. The dealer planned to send the junk to China where it would re-sell it for a handsome profit. The $100,000 windfall he paid for the junk was a much-needed infusion of cash.

I purchased $1.5 million in equipment that we would need to establish a full-fledged drilling operation — including slightly used heavy equipment and other vehicles that I bought in a fire sale in Hungary and had shipped by train to our site. (I earned some hard-to-get respect from OBN General Director Khramov when I told him of the equipment inventory: $9 million worth of equipment, including a small drilling rig, bought for $1.5 million. "You got a great deal," he said.)

By the time Well No. 128 came online, the oilfield looked like a national park with its natural setting in virgin forest, surrounded by mountains and accented by a small lake from a damned creek. The townspeople built a gazebo in the middle of the lake and made it accessible by a long wooden bridge.

"Well No. 128 looked like a national park by the time it came online."

The Baituganskoye field in summer.

The first BaiTex well, No. 128.

On November 11, 1995, Well No. 128, our first new well in the Baituganskoye area, began production. It was a huge milestone. The well was completed from Zavolzhsky Limestone (Lower Carboniferous) of Mississippian age, flowing 453 barrels of oil per day, 25.7 degrees gravity API through perforations at 4,225 feet.

One might wonder why our first well was numbered No. 128. The Russians had a system of numbering all the wells sequentially in a particular territory. If your first well was No. 128 on their master list for that territory that was the number you had to use.

In relatively short order, we had a total of 34 wells in production in the Baituganskoye field, including three new horizontal wells, using what was then new technology in Russia. Total field wells that were producing only 900 barrels of oil a day when BaiTex took over operations of the Baituganskoye field were producing 1,800-2,000 barrels per day 18 months later.

I was confident that the wells would return our investment thousands of times over their production life. The field operation, the management team, the oilfield employees, the revenue stream from the wells — typically the major challenges in oil projects — all proceeded as planned. But little did I know that our biggest challenges were yet to come.

"Little did I know our biggest challenges were yet to come."

CHAPTER 4

EVER-CHANGING RUSSIA

THE DAYS OF THE USSR WERE CLEARLY NUMBERED.

Even a year before my first trip to the Soviet Union in 1991, it was clear to my Russian colleagues that the days of the USSR were numbered. Far from certain were how the collapse would come about and what form of governance would replace the Soviet Union.

When Gorbachev took office in 1985, he had ignited the unraveling of the Soviet Union in what might be best described as a desperate attempt to "have one's cake and eat it, too."

"The Communist dominoes started to fall."

Naively, Gorbachev had wanted to preserve the old Soviet Union under Communist rule. But he believed that the only way to save it was to enact Western-style reforms aimed at cleaning up the country's pervasive corruption, and jump-starting its stalled economy that was burdened by unsustainable Cold War government spending.

His reforms made history, but not in the way he planned.

Since the 1917 Russian Revolution by the Bolsheviks ended the autocracy of the tsar who controlled and distributed all power and wealth, no single leader had brought about more change to the country than Joseph Stalin. As General Secretary of the Communist Party's Central Committee from 1922 until his death in 1953, Stalin used his office to brutally consolidate power after the death of Vladimir Lenin in 1924; Stalin gradually put down all opposition by executing thousands of political opponents, sending millions more to forced labor camps and deporting or exiling hundreds of thousands of others to remote areas of the Soviet Union.

Gorbachev pursued a different course — "*glasnost*." He opened things up (to a limit) and talked of removing the Soviet Union's main threats to the world. Light peeked through the cracks. However, to Gorbachev's great surprise his policies of openness and economic restructuring — "*perestroika*" — had the unintended consequence (from his perspective, we would learn later) of igniting freedom's fire, and popular uprisings soon followed throughout Eastern Europe. The Communist dominoes started to fall.

Yeltsin and Shock Therapy

After the U.S.S.R. split into 15 separate republics, President Boris Yeltsin led the Russian Federation, the largest of them. By this time, one-third of the Russian people lived in poverty. For decades, the Soviet government operated a centrally controlled system that not only set prices of common products, but its socialistic system severely limited the economic opportunities and civil freedoms of the Soviet people. Alcoholism was rampant throughout the country.

To address the sad legacy left by the Communist system, Yeltsin initiated a plan known as "shock therapy" — a set of policy changes that sought to convert the world's largest state-controlled economy into a market-oriented economy. The privatization of almost everything that had been controlled by the state — land, retail stores, factories, agriculture, oil — was a huge shock to Russians. Shock therapy also became the green light to foreign investors that Russia was open for business.

However, shock therapy created some unintended consequences. In the first month of the new policy, inflation caused prices to escalate 300 percent and by the end of 1992 nearly 2,600 percent. The result of such hyper-inflation was not only a severe devaluation of savings, salaries and pensions, but a rapid rise in energy and transportation costs that were still set by the government then, to a level four times higher than before shock therapy. Many factories were forced to shut down because the government subsidies that kept them open were eliminated, causing widespread unemployment.

Boris Yeltsin.

The Russian Mafia

But as destructive as some of these problems were, none was — in my view — as tragic as a new plague that developed in Russia, one that still infects the country today: the rise of the Russian mafia.

During Gorbachev's rule, corruption among Russian businessmen was prevalent and usually involved smuggling and reselling everyday goods, such as electronics and clothing. While the corruption was almost everywhere, it was minuscule compared to the corruption that took place during Yeltsin's reign.

When Yeltsin took over, the businessmen emerged almost overnight from nothing to powerful, rich entrepreneurs. The men, usually connected to government officials, learned how to work the new market-based economy to their advantage frequently using any means necessary to gain financial success. Often times, the corrupted officials allowed the new

"owners," sometimes called oligarchs, to either purchase cheaply or even take the property they wanted. If needed, officials were able to find excuses, even false ones, or loopholes to enable the oligarchs to stake their claim to a business or property. The oligarchs' financial and political influence impacted everyday business as they took control of successful projects throughout the country. In time, it appeared, Yeltsin and his oligarchs somehow found a way to control the new "free" market.

Because Russia had no rule of law, at least as we know it in the West — and because the Russian courts failed to enforce existing laws — the criminal pursuit of money and power negated the possibility of establishing a system needed to introduce private ownership and free markets in a rational way.

"I found myself stuck in the aisle of history."

Historically, Russia has always endured a mafia-like presence, notably in cities. Mafia thugs would stakeout street corners for the sale of foodstuffs and goods and beat up any newcomers who attempted to horn in on their territory. But during the chaos that ensued during "shock therapy," a new, more dangerous Russian mafia emerged and rapidly expanded its criminal operations — prostitution, gun and drug smuggling, black market commerce and shakedown practices. Throughout 1992, contract killings, bombings and kidnappings reached an all-time high as gangland murders became routine. A 1996 *Chicago Tribune* article reported, "Russian Interior Ministry officials commonly estimate that some 8,000 organized crime groups are vying for a stake in the nation's economy and that they already control nearly half of the country's stock exchanges and 60 percent of the banks. Officials say that 80 percent of all businesses pay some form of tribute to the ruthless gangsters."

The new criminal class infuriated the average Russian. Two years after the fall of the Soviet Union, public opinion polls showed Russians yearning for the stability, predictability and general safety that they perceived that Communism provided them — even as evidence showed former Communists were benefitting financially from Russia's attempted transition to free markets.

Russia had free-fallen into the economic, social and political chaos that characterized the country through the 1990s. More than

two dozen Russian bankers were murdered, along with more than a few "foreigners." In 1996, a Tulsa businessman named Paul Tatum, the joint venture co-owner of a major new Moscow hotel, who had publicly complained about his treatment by a Russian business partner from Chechnya, was assassinated at a Moscow subway station while Tatum's bevy of bodyguards stood by. Never captured, the hitman was widely assumed to work for the Chechen partner. Days after Tatum's death, the partner and the Moscow city government quickly took over complete control of the hotel joint venture.

I found myself not solely on the front row of history, but stuck in its aisle. I had become an unwitting participant in an ever-changing transformation from Communism to the present Russian system of crony-elite ownership and control, a kind of contemporary feudalism, in which economic oligarchs rule in the name of "sovereign democracy," while skimming off profits, hiding assets and eliminating liabilities.

Financial Crisis in Russia

Nineteen ninety-seven and 1998 were among the worst years of my time in Russia. Ironically, the reasons had little to do with the BaiTex oil operation; it ran like a Swiss watch, except for licensing transfer and other political issues.

My problem was financial: I was nearly out of operating cash as the Russians were not honoring our joint-venture contract as to the payments for oil produced. In a few months, I would have no choice but to shut down operations.

Further complicating matters was the 1998 financial crisis in Russia, which saw the country default on its debts. Declining productivity, an exchange rate between the ruble and foreign

Typical open air market with Russians trying to sell their family's secondhand clothing to make ends meet, 1991.

"RUSSIA WAS DEFAULTING ON ITS DEBTS AND I WAS NEARLY OUT OF CASH."

currencies that was fixed artificially high to avoid public turmoil, and a chronic fiscal deficit triggered the crisis. It hit some of the oligarchs hard, and those whose holdings were based on banking lost much of their fortunes. Russia emerged from bankruptcy in three years, largely due to a sustained spike in the price of oil, which Russia was exporting in huge volumes — among them the several thousand barrels our wells produced each day.

With recovery under way in Russia, on December 31, 1999, Yeltsin made a surprise announcement. He had resigned and Prime Minister Vladimir Putin had taken over as acting president, with elections due to take place on March 26, 2000. Russia needed to enter the new century with new political leaders, Yeltsin said, concluding: "I want to beg forgiveness for your dreams that never came true. And also I would like to beg forgiveness not to have justified your hopes."

Russia Wasn't All Work

Throughout our time in Russia, Leah and I struggled not knowing what the next day would bring. Day-by-day new challenges presented themselves that we did not anticipate; to us, Russia was an adventure of a lifetime. Leah summed it up well in a letter to our family and friends, "It [Russia] is not an easy place to do business. After a huge investment of time, energy and money, we are finding the greatest rewards are not always measured in monetary success although that would be nice, too. Rather, our lives have been enriched and broadened greatly by wonderful adventures, deep and touching friendships, and a chance to offer help to a nation of people who are intelligent and talented, but have been held back in so many ways. At times, I become fearful wondering how and where all this will end."

Even though business in Russia was taxing, we made time to escape the stress by exploring this new and very foreign land. We had some contacts with the West through our expat friends and we enjoyed regular worship at Moscow's

Jerry flying command in a small Russian Yakovlev Yak-40 three-engine jet on a trip out to view a Russian oilfield, September 20, 1991.

Leah flying co-pilot during the flight out to look at the oilfields.

only Anglican congregation. Through the church I was blessed to fellowship regularly with a group of expat businessmen, which was instrumental to my growth while in Russia.

We have always possessed a deep appreciation for the arts and that did not diminish while we were in Russia. We took full advantage of our time there by regularly attending music concerts and perusing the local markets for paintings and antiques. In fact, Leah developed such a love for Russian art that she established a successful business, importing Russian paintings into the U.S.

Throughout our time in Russia, we enjoyed learning the culture and meeting the people. This was a far cry from the Texas life we had grown comfortable with during the past 30 years. In one sense we made Russia our second home.

The Duffle Bag

Despite our growing love of the culture, we still had a tremendous number of "unknowns" we regularly faced. So much so, that Leah and I kept a black duffle bag in our apartment, which we set aside to carry rugs, paintings and small antiques if we ever needed to quickly leave Moscow for safety reasons, or the day it became clear that our Russian adventure was over.

On occasions when money became extra tight or when it seemed all hope had faded for a positive resolution to a deal-killing problem, I packed the duffle bag with our belongings. Upon seeing the duffle arrive in Dallas, Leah would ask if we were leaving Russia for good.

"Yes, I think maybe this time we're through," I said. "It looks like we may not make it."

The black duffle bag made the round trip between Moscow and Dallas and then back to Moscow three times during the 16 years I worked in Russia.

Arriving at our Dallas home from the airport, I'd toss the duffle bag on the floor in the hall near our front door, go upstairs and go to bed.

My daughters would call Leah the next morning and ask, "Is Dad back?"

"Yes," Leah would answer. "He arrived last night."

A second question would follow immediately. "Did he bring the black duffle bag?"

"The duffle bag became a symbol of our Russian adventure ending."

Irina translating for Jerry as he addresses Russian staff at the oilfield.

Medical Attention Notice

Doing business in Russia was unlike anything I have ever experienced. Learning to live and work in a foreign culture brought about many challenges and at times potential safety issues. Being an American citizen afforded me many safeguards that helped my family adapt more easily to me living in a foreign country.

As a precaution and to help insure my safety while in Russia, I carried a medical attention notice. The card, which was written in English on one side and Russian on the other, said "I am an American. I need medical help. Please call the American Medical Center." It served as an emergency safeguard in case I experienced a medical emergency or life-threatening situation.

For quick identification the card included my name and contact information, as well as the name and information about my company and various Russian associates to contact in case of an emergency. Of course, my contacts listed included my employees Irina Kapina and Valery Yudin, as well as my Russian confidante George Gogonenkov. Thankfully, I never had to use my medical attention notice while in Russia; but it definitely gave me peace of mind knowing that in a crisis I would get the attention and help I needed and my family would be contacted immediately.

Contract Not Being Met

Not long after beginning operations in Russia, my company and other foreign joint ventures ran into an enduring problem that will keep Russia from fully participating in the developed world's arena of business and finance: a virtual absence of the rule of law.

Approvals granted by government bureaucracy one day were rejected the next. Applications for permits went unanswered because no one knew what the new regulations might be. "Don't know." "Come back tomorrow." "Come back next month." "Maybe." These were the bywords of business in Russia immediately following the collapse of Communism and the Soviet Union. The bureaucratic shuffling and stalling went on and on, causing deal after deal to crash, along with my chances to hang on to my much underfinanced company.

Into this vacuum stepped a Russian mafia-style brand of business, a kind of lawlessness that made commercial life a rollercoaster of hit and miss, hope and despair. Russian courts — when judges were courageous enough to act — were virtually powerless to enforce judgments, leaving native "partners" free to continue extorting, falsifying and otherwise thieving. Not only did this dysfunctional environment make it virtually impossible for my little company to get anything accomplished, it cast a pall of mistrust and discouragement over the whole of Russia.

"Russians expect lies, theft and brutality and are seldom disappointed."

Jerry, Valery and Irina are among the visitors touring an oil treatment center at the Baituganskoye field.

Absent the rule of law in Russia, anything could happen and often did. The man who was my benevolent Russian friend, George Gogonenkov, told me, "Russians always expect three things from government — lies, theft and brutality — and they're seldom disappointed."

The biggest problem I had — and had no control over whatsoever — was that I couldn't get the Russians with whom I was working to observe the terms we had agreed to in our contract. OBN failed to transfer the license required for BaiTex to sell the oil our wells were producing. And, a large problem both parties had to endure was that the Russian government kept changing the rules we were to play by!

Day-to-day, the crisis played out like a bad soap opera — but the drama was all too real.

In Russia, you're out of luck without a government license. Unlike in the United States, all minerals — diamonds, gas, oil, coal and everything in the ground — belongs to the state. The state will grant or sell licenses, issued through various government ministries, to extract a particular mineral in a specific geographic area. While the minerals are underground, they're state property. Brought to the surface — at your expense and risk — they become your property. To sell them legally on the domestic or international market, you need a license — or face time in *tyur'ma* (prison).

Under the terms of our 50-50 partnership agreement, BaiTex and OBN would split profits equally, and OBN would immediately transfer to BaiTex the license required by the Russian government to sell oil to domestic and world markets. The contract stipulated that the company would use "all best efforts" to transfer the government license to BaiTex, so we could start not only recouping our investment, but take profit due us. From the beginning of our partnership, OBN would neither split the profits with us equally nor transfer the license to BaiTex, a clear violation of contract terms. As long as OBN kept the license, while we made the investment and did the work, OBN sold the oil at market price, which, by the year 2000, had climbed to about $40 a barrel. OBN paid us $4.39 a barrel, which they considered an "operating fee" paid to a contractor, not a 50-percent partner. The $4.39 a barrel fee was far from an arbitrary figure. The fee — keenly arrived at by some OBN accountant — was precisely how much income BaiTex needed to keep the lights on and produce the oil.

Adding great injury to insult in the middle of this, the Russian government passed a law in 1996 that prohibited the transfer of oil licenses from one party to another. I could not believe it! The law was quickly repealed after foreign oil companies who were investing billions in the Russian oil industry — giants like ExxonMobil

The drilling floor of a BaiTex well in Russia.

Jerry with a group visiting the future site for a petroleum plant in Russia.

and British Petroleum — announced that they would pull out of Russia if the law was not rescinded.

Until the license was transferred, OBN knew it could continue to pay BaiTex the $4.39 fee. Once the license was transferred to BaiTex, OBN would have to pay our company half of the proceeds — a transaction, needless to say, that OBN was not eager to conclude. While I have never fully figured out how much OBN had gotten away with through this scheme — it makes my blood boil even now to put a number on it — I'm pretty certain it was $50-plus million.

Our contract with OBN had been written with great precision over a period of several months beginning in 1993, with the help of attorneys in Dallas, Washington D.C. and Moscow. Our Russian partners, who had never done business before with an American company, spent months to painstakingly review each word in our partnership agreement. The contract, both parties agreed in writing, was unaffected by the late 2000 purchase of OBN by the giant Tyumen Oil Company of Western Siberia (TNK), one of Russia's largest and newest privately-owned companies. With a reputation for being rough and tough, TNK was owned by a consortium comprised of some of Russia's most powerful oligarchs.

Trying to Survive

By the year 2000, while people around the globe prepared to celebrate the arrival of the third Millennium, I was clinging to hope that I would survive financially to see it. After nearly nine years of doing business in Russia, I still had no license to sell the oil that my company had produced. TNK — the large oil company that now owned OBN and which had posted $2 billion in revenue the year before — could have easily accommodated the contract requirements of our joint venture but had not.

Call me naïve — heck, foolish might be more accurate, according to most — I dug in my heels, believing that "right" would win out, and the promised license would eventually be transferred to BaiTex. No evidence to support my position existed. In fact, evidence abounded that the opposite was true. Of the 340-plus foreign joint ventures approved and registered by the Russian government in 1993, only three were left standing. My little company was one of the three. All the others had pulled out in despair, anger and, often enough, fear — leaving trainloads of equipment and tens of millions of dollars in capital investment.

What was I to do? I did the only thing I knew would work.

I engaged a practice that my ancestors had passed along to me — a habit that I'm certain Peter Fullinwider, my great-great-grandfather, embraced as he rode in the pitch black of the wee hours through the Indian Tejas territory.

I prayed.

"God, you've protected me here so far. I've been in really dirty places. I have drunk way too much vodka. I've eaten some terrible stuff, but I've never been sick to speak of thanks to your protection. I still have my energy and my health. But maybe I'm through here. I don't think I can resolve the recent problems thrown upon our path. But if you make an opening, I'll step through it. And if you don't, that's OK, too."

I was about to find out my situation in Russia was really deteriorating.

"God, if you make
an opening,
I'll step through it
And if you don't,
that's OK, too."

CHAPTER 5

THE CLEANER

LISTEN TO ME, WE ARE IN VERY SERIOUS TROUBLE.

In late November 2000, I picked up the phone ringing in our hotel room in St. Petersburg where Leah and I had gone for a few days to rendezvous with family on a sightseeing trip before returning to Texas for Christmas. On the other end, I heard the breathless and panicked voice of our Russian General Manager, Valery Yudin.

"I thought they were going to kill me."

— Valery Yudin

"Jerry, I thought they were going to kill me when I would not sign over our operation," he shouted over the phone, his thick Russian-accented English barely understandable.

"Oh, God, these people, they gave me this contract to sign," he said.

Dumbfounded by Yudin's call, I tried to slow the pace of the conversation.

"What people?" "What contract?" I asked Yudin. "Where are you?"

Gradually I started to get the straight story from Yudin. He was a seasoned Russian oil executive whose late father, a highly-regarded jurist, had defended some of the most prominent of the accused in Stalin's 1937 show trials of utterly innocent "traitors," all of whom were subsequently executed. Growing up watching his father speak truth to power, and narrowly escaping with his life, gave Yudin, a short, stocky Jew with intense black eyes and caterpillar eyebrows, the gift of a keen sensitivity to approaching danger.

Now, here he was on the other end of the phone line 1,300 miles away in Orenburg scared senseless. He had my full attention.

"Listen to me, we're in very serious trouble, Jerry," he said.

Frantic Call from Valery

As the details emerged, it became clear to me that a showdown nearly 10 years in the making had arrived. By the year 2000, TNK was ready to reorganize OBN, as large conglomerates often want to do for more profit. To accomplish the job, OBN's new ownership sent Victor Kruger, a middle management member of TNK from Nizhnevartovsk in Western Siberia, to OBN headquarters to "clean out" any remaining "contractors" who might be clogging the works.

Summoned to the "urgent" meeting on November 26, 2000, at OBN headquarters, Yudin and other contractors involved in business with OBN were told by Kruger that, as of December 1, all "operating agreements" would be unilaterally terminated. OBN (under new TNK management) would then rent or buy their equipment, at a price set by TNK, and take over their employees and their businesses.

At the meeting, Kruger was joined by his top deputy, Yuri Takidze, a smart, tough Chechen in his thirties along with a small security force armed with Russian Makarov pistols and Kalashnikov machine guns. While the security force was present to protect Kruger, it didn't take much for the dozen or so local contractors at the meeting to imagine them as a firing squad.

116

The contractors were handed termination contracts and told to sign them. All but one did so. The exception was Valery Yudin. Yudin attempted to explain that BaiTex has an ownership position in the oilfield — not a contractor position, but Takidze interrupted. TNK had plenty of money without the investment from Texas, he told Yudin. And, he added, Halliburton, the American oilfield technology and service company, would provide access to new Western technologies.

When Yudin refused to pick up the pen to sign the termination documents after explaining that he was not owner of BaiTex and had no authority to execute the document, they pounded the desk, shouted and cursed at Yudin — a drama played out under the gaze of guards with machine guns.

"The new owners…" a nearly breathless Yudin told me. "They told me I had to sign over ownership of BaiTex or they wouldn't be responsible for the consequences. They said our deal was off — all of our contracts were null and void. We are to just leave, get out. Leave all of our equipment. We would get no compensation. They yelled and cursed and slammed their fists on the tables. Jerry, I was afraid they were going to kill me."

Instinctively, I shot back a reply.

"If you had signed those documents, I would have killed you myself," I told Yudin. "For now, you get out of there. Talk to no one. I'll meet you back in Moscow in a couple of days, and we'll figure this out."

"IF YOU HAD SIGNED THOSE DOCUMENTS, I WOULD HAVE KILLED YOU MYSELF."

Change of Plans

Before I hung up from the call with Yudin, I already knew my next move. I was no contractor for OBN or TNK. I was an owner with a 50 percent stake in the company, an owner who hadn't been paid his fair share of revenues and profits for six years. I had hung in with Russia when all but a few firms had bailed out. I knew Russia to be a country where the balance of rational and irrational seemed steadfastly weighed more toward the latter, where more seemed to hang on relationships, coincidence and something approaching the unknowable — half luck and half providence — but I wasn't about to abandon the project.

I may be 9,000 miles from home, I thought, but I possessed valuable knowledge of virtually all phases of the upstream oil industry. My acquaintance with geology, geophysics, engineering and logistics, in addition to my legal, financial and promotional experience in Texas, had, so far, helped me feel my way through a great tangle of problems while virtually alone in Russia's vastness.

I knew I would have to dig deep to face this latest crisis in Russia — which may very well become my last stand. But I knew the crude truth of my oil business in Russia. I felt I must not fail because I'd be likely ruined if I did. Growing up in Texas, hearing the stories of my ancestors and their accomplishments, and having achieved most of the goals I had set for my own life, had taught me this: you can't know the future in advance – but you can experience it by stepping into it.

I would go to Orenburg to meet with the Russian thug whom Yudin told me tried to shake him down for a fast signature, which may well have ended our Russian business.

I told Yudin goodbye and hung up the phone. I wrote down the man's name: "Victor Kruger."

I thought to myself, "What's Victor Kruger going to do anyway, kill me?"

I turned to speak to my wife, clearly eager for a debriefing. "Change in plans," I told her. "The mob has arrived."

"WHAT'S HE GOING
TO DO ANYWAY,
KILL ME?

CHANGE IN
PLANS,
THE MOB
HAS ARRIVED."

"The tall Texan and Russian cleaner were on a collision course."

Preparing to Meet the Cleaner

In the few days between Yudin's call and the trip to confront the toughs sent to shut down BaiTex, I had engaged in a little "spying" of my own. I knew, for example, that the TNK mid-level manager, Victor Kruger, with whom we would meet — the man who yelled and cursed at Yudin — was an oil and gas veteran with a degree in engineering. Kruger had worked his way up in the TNK organization, starting as a mechanic on oil rigs in Russia's Far East energy operation under the most extreme weather conditions.

I knew he had been sent by the new TNK owners during the takeover of OBN's daily operations in Orenburg to get rid of contractors who were not part of the TNK network — a task with a euphemistic title that translated as a "cleaner." Cleaners were sent by new owners to ruthlessly nullify contracts, fire crooks and restructure the accounting department. The "cleanup" typically meant shutting down the theft and graft involving contractors such as truckers, suppliers, pipefitters and others who might have been splitting substantial payments for fictitious contracts with the old company bosses.

Rather than try to sort out which contractors were doing the jobs for which they were hired and which were faking them, the new owners found it simpler to fire them all, then install their own contractors offering better deals. TNK was intent on ridding OBN's old guard thieves in order to appoint their own. That made the job of a cleaner in West Siberia a risky business. Newspapers carried stories about cleaners who had been assaulted and, in some cases, murdered. Most cleaners travelled with bodyguards.

The tall Texan and the Russian cleaner were on a collision course, and the last one standing stood to gain — or lose — possibly millions of dollars. And to hear Yudin tell the story, Victor Kruger intended to win the draw.

A Rough Trip

The 90-minute flight from Moscow to Orenburg was turbulent — a sign of changing winter jet streams and, I feared, the days to come — a bumpy ride that seemed an appropriate portent given the pending showdown the next day with my "partner" at the giant oil firm TNK who had been sent to shut down my Russian operation and send me back to Texas empty-handed.

It was a bitterly cold day when we stepped from the aging Aeroflot jet's metal stairway and onto the asphalt tarmac at the Tsentralny Airport 20 miles from Orenburg. Chilly as it was, the early December weather would be no match for the heavy Siberian snows that would arrive with a vengeance in a few weeks' time.

Penetrating my heavy clothing — heck, my 72-year-old bones — the cold settled in for the ride on the unheated shuttle bus that would ferry us to the unheated and darkened terminal where we waited for our luggage. "Why can't these Russians get some more heaters and light bulbs around here," I thought. Joining me on the trip to Orenburg were Yudin, my trusted translator Victor Nikitin and Henk Jelsma, the Dutchman I had hired as president and chief operating officer of VF-Russia, Inc., the parent company of BaiTex.

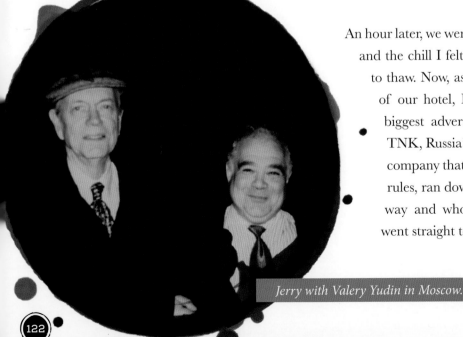

An hour later, we were riding in a heated taxi, and the chill I felt so deeply finally began to thaw. Now, as our cab pulled in front of our hotel, I was about to face my biggest adversary to date in Russia: TNK, Russia's third-largest oil firm, a company that seemed to make its own rules, ran down anyone who got in its way and whose ties to the Kremlin went straight to the top.

Jerry with Valery Yudin in Moscow.

The Hurried Walk

After a restless night in the grim hotel — owned by OBN — I awoke on December 5, 2000, and dressed in my characteristic blue pinstriped suit, ironed shirt and red tie. While I am a proud Texan, I am not a rancher and don't affect the look: "boots and cowboy hat."

As we began to walk the few blocks to OBN headquarters for the meeting with Kruger, I noticed Nikitin, Yudin and Jelsma were having a hard time keeping up with me. Adrenalin had apparently made my normally rigorous walking pace even faster.

As we strode through the small square in front of the block-long headquarters of Orenburgneft, built in the 1940s, I noticed the dingy landscape, the unkempt gardens and the shuttered fountain. Winter had arrived in Orenburg.

By 2000, Orenburg had not yet benefitted from the prosperity that was visible in other major Russian cities. Although the situation is now changed, back then in Orenburg there were no apparent signs of wealth — no luxury car dealers offering brands like Mercedes-Benz, Jaguar or Cadillac as there were in Moscow.

That's why I was surprised to see, as we approached the steps to the entrance of the OBN building, a new Mercedes limousine, parked on the street.

"Good grief, look at that car," I said to Nikitin.

"What is that?" my interpreter asked.

"It's a Mercedes limo, it's new and it's armored. You can tell by the way it sits low on its chassis," I said.

Then, I noticed the hood ornament. Perched on the front fender of the Mercedes was a young man dressed in jeans, a black leather jacket and a cap — the Mercedes' bodyguard. He was armed with a Kalashnikov AK-47, the automatic weapon of choice used by the Russian military, and a favorite of Russian mafia and the bodyguards of those in power — men like Victor Kruger.

Gauging the Situation

Entering the building, the usually quiet lobby was full of people, among them a security guard I recognized — a Russian version of Barney Fife. Dressed in his standard blue pants and light blue shirt adorned with badge and medals, the guard carried a small-caliber 9mm Makarov pistol in a side holster. On this day, however, the familiar guard had backup: two other guards, positioned in opposite corners of the lobby and shouldering Kalashnikovs, stood sentry.

As we approached the dark staircase to the second floor executive offices of OBN — the building had no elevators and the hallways were dimly lit as usual — I told Yudin to scout around the back halls. "Talk to some people and see what you can find out," I told him. Nikitin, Jelsma and I headed up the stairs.

Reaching a dingy landing where the stairway turned a blind corner, I almost collided with another guard standing in the shadowy corner, a gun butt sticking out of his jacket; the guard reeked of vodka and cigarettes.

Arriving to the anteroom of the executive suites, we were greeted by a scene straight from a grade-B foreign movie. Sitting in chairs lining the walls were a dozen or so middle-aged men, leaning forward, heads down, twirling their caps — and appearing frightened as all get out. I guessed that they were more contractors awaiting the ax.

"HOLY SMOKES."

Meeting the Cleaner

Within in a few minutes, Nikitin, Jelsma and I were ushered through a double-door entrance into a private office — the second door unlocked only after the first was locked behind us — and that's when we were greeted by the Russian giant guarding the door. "Holy smokes," I thought.

Yudin had not caught up with us yet when we were taken to Kruger's office. Good thing. He would have been scared witless by the 6-foot-5, 300-pound Russian guard who greeted us with unfriendly scowls, a giant fellow with a long scar on his face who seemed to have no neck, his ears disappearing into his massive shoulders. The guard wore ill-fitting clothing, and through a gap where he hadn't been able to button his coat across his broad chest, I could see the butt of a gun. I thought I had seen the man before: he looked like the character "Jaws" in the James Bond movie, except this tough-guy's teeth were gold instead of steel.

Entering the spacious private office, I saw Kruger, dressed immaculately, sitting behind a large T-shaped desk as his deputy, Takidze, stood near him. Each man sucked on a Marlboro. The desk Kruger occupied connected to a narrow, longish table that branched out at a 90-degree angle to form a "T." Multiple sets of rotary dial phones adorned the desktop — symbols of importance in Russia; the more phones on the boss's desk, the more important the boss appeared.

Kruger sat at the top of the "T" — the power position among Russian executives — from the President of Russia, to the president of the grocery store chain, to the head of OBN; the big bosses all had such furniture designed to show subordinates who was boss, a theater prop dating back centuries to show power. Two other men were in the room. One stood behind us, holstering a Makarov pistol; the other, stationed in the corner, held a Kalashnikov.

The Silent Standoff

Just as we were seated, before a word was spoken, Yudin arrived in the office and sat to my right. [He whispered] "Everyone's too scared to talk to me."

No one spoke in the office, either. The standoff was underway.

I glanced across the table and winked at Nikitin, a signal to follow my lead. In a few moments, the silence of the room was broken by a slight repetitive sound. It took me a moment to identify the source: Kruger. He was nervously clicking his fingernails on the desk.

Tactically, both of us knew to wait for the other to speak first. The first man to show his cards would likely lose. Game on.

Kruger folded first.

"Why do you want to see me?" he demanded.

Through Nikitin, I explained to Kruger who I was, and I outlined the terms of our joint venture with OBN. I also told Kruger that I had heard from Yudin that he had tried to have certain contracts cancelled or suspended related to our joint venture.

"We're like a broom," Kruger said of TNK management's new approach to those doing business with OBN. "We will clean up the old business and start from scratch. No more secret dealings and corruptions."

Then, without missing a beat, Kruger told me that he had some contracts for me to sign, and pushed two copies across the desk, one in Russian, the other in English.

"We will clean up. No more secret dealings and corruptions."

— Victor Kruger

Orenburgneft (OBN) Headquarters in Orenburg in Southern Russia.

"Sign them," he ordered. "Sign them now."

Calmly, I replied: "Do you mind if I read them first?"

"Fine," he retorted. "But nothing will change."

I had to give the cleaner credit for the straightforward nature of the contract he urgently wanted my signature on. The contract said that our agreement with OBN was no longer in the interest of the parties to continue and, thereby, null and void. I was free, as were all BaiTex employees, to leave Russia with no payment for our efforts or for our equipment. In short, "the deal is off, leave Russia and goodbye."

Defending Our Contract

After reading the contract, I set the document on the table and looked Kruger directly in the eye. I had worked too hard and invested too much time, talent and treasure to walk from this deal, let alone be pushed out by some mid-level bureaucrat who had no concept of rule of law. As Leah would remind me from time to time, our retirement was at risk — our whole livelihood — tied to success in Russia. We could not fail now and I would give it my all to see that we did not lose this battle with Kruger.

Nikitin translated word-for-word as I began to speak.

"My business is legal," I said. "It's one of the Pioneer Priority Projects so designated by Vice President Gore and Prime Minister Chernomyrdin, and it is an honor to represent the United States in this way."

"So, no, I will not sign your papers."

Out of the corner of my eye, I noticed the bodyguard in the corner become noticeably agitated. He gripped the Kalashnikov so tightly his knuckles turned white.

Unimpressed by my reply, Kruger seemed almost unaware of our agreement with OBN. After a short pause, I continued, politely, to explain the situation to Kruger, who abruptly cut me off.

"You can explain, but not now and not to me. I've heard enough. No more joint ventures," Kruger said.

I pushed the contracts — unsigned, of course — back to Kruger, who instantly became agitated. Suddenly, Takidze, the Chechen, began speaking to me in a highly annoyed tone of voice, telling me that our contract with OBN was illegal, that TNK management had every right to cancel it right there and then.

"YOU CAN EXPLAIN, BUT NOT NOW AND NOT TO ME. I'VE HEARD ENOUGH."

— VICTOR KRUGER

"You may have heard of our attorney. I believe he's your lawyer too."

Throughout the display of unprofessional and rude behavior, I remained calm, cool and collected (although I am amazed I could pull it off), which appeared only to aggravate the cleaner and his assistant all the more as evidenced by their shouting, cursing and hammering with the flats of their hands on the desk.

"Victor, what are they saying," I asked Nikitin.

"You don't want to know," he replied.

By now, both armed guards had joined the Russian theater troupe in their display of righteous indignation; the guards shuffled their feet, grimaced and generally appeared menacing, as if hoping that one of us unarmed businessmen would make a threatening move to justify their unloading a burst of gun fire in our direction.

None of us took the bait, of course. I repeated — or tried to through their shouts and curses — that our contract was legal. I told Kruger that I would have our lawyers in Moscow and Washington contact him.

"You may have heard of our attorney," I said, pausing for dramatic effect. "His name is Valery Volkov. I believe he's your lawyer, too." The implication I sought to convey is that a contract drawn up by Volkov for one client would be respected by another client. Kruger brushed off the words, repeating that TNK management no longer needed BaiTex.

"Yes, when the deal was inked, Orenburgneft needed people like you. Now, we have everything we need, and I've never seen your contracts." Kruger retorted in a rude tone, oblivious to the binding nature of legal agreements.

Making My Move

Now, I made my move.

From my briefcase, I slowly and in full view of the guards, removed my own copies of the original contract. I told Kruger that BaiTex had honored its part of the deal and that it was Orenburgneft who owed BaiTex $5 million for oil delivered and services rendered but not paid for, and that it was OBN who had defaulted on its agreement to transfer the license to the joint venture company.

I pushed copies of the original agreement across the desk to Kruger, one in Russian and the other in English, and turned to a paragraph in the Russian version that I had paper-clipped and said, "Here's where OBN agreed to transfer the license."

Kruger stared at the document, a scowl crossing his face.

It was time to go.

Leaving the papers on Kruger's desk, I stood up, politely said goodbye and left the office with my associates in tow.

A workover rig in the BaiTex oilfield in Russia.

Making it Out Alive

As we walked out of the building, Nikitin told me he had never seen a person so cool and calm under such pressure from Russian heavies. Then he asked, "Do you think we're going to get out of this town alive?"

I knew that there was a chance following the meeting that TNK might immediately move to take over the BaiTex field. I suspected that they might even remove all of our oil equipment. But I didn't think they would take me out of the picture.

"Yes, we will," I said. "It's just Russian theater. They are trying to run me off. They're doing this all over Russia, and most people bail out."

"Not me."

Victor Kruger's blustering threats had shaken me, but the unpleasant episode also toughened my resolve to move forward quickly, carefully and decisively to see our investment of work, time, talent and money in the BaiTex project through to a positive conclusion.

I began my work in Russia before there was an independent Russia, and I would not be sidetracked by a mid-level bureaucrat who had no respect for rule of law, and thereby abandon the Russian employees who counted on me to make a living, not to mention my personal stake in the venture. To Kruger and TNK, I was a minor contractual problem to be eliminated on its course of rapid expansion as Russia, overall, continued on the path to achieve status as the world's leading oil producer.

Following my showdown with Kruger in Orenburg, Yudin and Nikitin worried for my personal safety, as did my wife Leah, whom I briefed on the situation. "They probably wouldn't have shot you right there," she said, "but you might have been 'accidently' run over by a truck when you left the meeting."

I wasn't worried about staying alive. I was deeply concerned about keeping the ownership of my company and the Baituganskoye oil project. Bald takeovers were typical of large Russian companies owned by oligarchs who were out to (and continue to) poison opportunities for business competitors, foreign investors and the Russian people who need and want jobs. Companies far larger than VF-Russia had found their businesses expropriated through a series of complex and — from the perspective of Western business culture — indefensibly crooked maneuvers.

Networking to Save BaiTex

In the immediate days following the meeting with Kruger, I began loading and locking my own intellectual arsenal to engage in battle with the Russian oil giant, TNK. Not only did I alert my lawyers on two continents, I made a list of contacts in Russia, England and Texas whose help I would need to win.

My first call, to lawyer Valery Volkov in Moscow who had been working with our firm for five years, provided instant relief and hope. Volkov, whom I had mentioned to Kruger during our meeting in Orenburg, was managing partner of Russia's most prestigious law firm. Well-connected politically, Volkov wrote widely on a variety of legal subjects for reputable, highly-regarded publications in Russia. TNK had placed him on retainer after he was already our lawyer of record, although Volkov would later tell me that TNK had never asked him to do anything.

"If you have a legal beef with TNK, I'm your man," Volkov told me over the phone. Upon

"Can you call the Queen and have her tell the Russians they can't muscle me around?"

hearing these first words of support, I almost became teary as I did not think Volkov would stick with me against the powerful TNK.

Next, I phoned Gary Fitzgerald, the managing director of one of our investors in London, the British Framlington Russian Investment Fund, chaired by Lord Geoffrey Howe. "Gary, we're in trouble here," I told him. "We need help, and we need it now. They're trying to kick us out of Russia. Lord Howe has connections. Can you get him to call someone and have them tell the Russians that they can't muscle me around? We're about to lose our shirt."

Gary assured me that he would pursue contacts to register their deep concern over TNK's bully behavior.

Next, I phoned Don Zarin, our lawyer in Washington, D.C., who had worked for many years as a lawyer in the U.S. Department of Commerce and who had many contacts at the highest levels of Russian business and government. Zarin delighted me when he volunteered to advise his Russian contacts that "Fullinwider and VF-Russia were not the type to go away quietly and his contracts should be upheld."

And, I phoned my good friend and Russian advisor, Robert Jenkins, who divided his time between London and Moscow. Over the years, Robert and I had enjoyed many dinners together when our wives had not joined us on our trips to Moscow. He knew about all of our problems in Russia. No shrinking violet, Robert, who spoke fluent Russian, said he would simply phone his contacts at TNK.

Over the phone, Jenkins told his contact: "You know, people can't treat Fullinwider this way. His project has been named a Pioneer Priority Project — one of only five in the whole country. He's a strong, able American businessman who has completed his share of the contract and your people need to do their share. You can't brush him off."

As the year 2000 ended and the new year began, I continued behind the scenes to apply pressure on TNK to honor their contractual obligations. Yet, it was clear TNK either knew nothing about the BaiTex contract or, more likely, didn't care about honoring the agreement.

"Fullinwider and VF Russia would not go away quietly."

— Don Zarin

Friendly Negotiations

In February of 2001, Kruger's deputy, Takidze, issued orders to the TNK General Counsel's office to find a legal way to break the joint venture agreement with BaiTex.

Meantime, Kruger continued trying to browbeat Yudin to sign off on changes to the BaiTex agreement, which would have immediately terminated our Russian operations.

Fortunately, ignorance and incompetence joined forces in the TNK legal department and Takidze's efforts failed miserably. At the time, Russian attorneys not only were generally unschooled in contract law, they simply didn't know how to formulate a legal plan to get TNK out of the BaiTex contract.

Word finally reached Kruger from the top that "some guy named Fullinwider" was stirring up trouble by claiming TNK owed him money and a license to sell oil because of some pre-existing contract with OBN. Kruger was furious. In a

letter to me, Kruger instructed me to speak only to him from now on or "there would be no more friendly negotiations." Of course, there hadn't been "friendly" anything, let alone "negotiations."

I wrote a return letter, telling Kruger that I would be content to meet with him about BaiTex matters as long as progress was made to resolve outstanding issues in a businesslike manner. I further stipulated that any resolution must not prejudice the legal or economic positions of either party.

"The price for the oil would be 'determined' later."

On February 19, 2001, about 11 weeks after our initial meeting in Orenburg, the team from BaiTex — me, Jelsma, Yudin, Zarin and Volkov — met in OBN's Moscow office with the TNK team, Kruger, Takidze, their lawyer, Dimitry Eicher, and others I didn't know. Although the team from TNK seemed stiff and distant, the meeting was cordial. It began with an offer from Kruger to back fund — and resume payments on — current oil runs, which TNK had stopped making the previous September. The price for the oil would be "determined" later, Kruger said.

When our side pressed for an estimate right then, Kruger said OBN was currently selling oil to its parent company, TNK, for about $7.50 a barrel even though domestic marketing prices were in the $18 to $20 per barrel range — cutting us out of millions of dollars in profit over a year's time.

To add insult to injury, Kruger said any payments would be made in rubles and labeled as a "service fee" — a continuation of the argument he first made at our December meeting. Kruger refused to acknowledge that we were a partner in a joint venture with TNK, that we owned a 50 percent stake in the Baituganskoye oilfield, and that we were entitled by contract to be paid in U.S. dollars.

A well in Baituganskoye field sheltered by a protected forest.

Then, Kruger proceeded to attempt to extort us. BaiTex, he said, would have no hope of receiving the license to sell oil promised in the 1993 agreement — and no guarantee it ever would be transferred — unless the company showed TNK what new technologies it was using to extract so much oil from its BaiTex field compared to what OBN well technologies were yielding in its nearby fields.

We decided to engage Kruger in his game. We could always resort to a lawsuit, although I was far from confident that would end well for us.

On March 13, a summary description of the technical means used by BaiTex at the Baituganskoye field was delivered to TNK. During a conference call on March 21, Kruger complained that the technical documents were too general and failed to provide the means for TNK to calculate cash flow projections for their wells.

Smelling a rat who wanted to steal our technologies without any resolution to our BaiTex agreement — let alone compensation for our assistance on improving well production — our team included cash flow projections in the follow-up communiqué, but we withheld detailed descriptions of the technologies used to deliver them. In our follow-up letter, we made it very clear that TNK would have to pay us all past-due compensation, set a fair price for current oil runs and provide an acceptable timeline for transferring the license to the BaiTex field.

Pressing On

On April 17, 2001, the two sides met again in Moscow. After some aggressive negotiations, Kruger agreed to pay us $6.48 per barrel for unpaid oil runs. At the time, oil was selling in the Russian domestic markets of up to $20 per barrel, meaning we were still being shortchanged millions of dollars in revenue. We would not agree to this price.

Three days later, the two sides agreed to meet in Orenburg to discuss the technical knowledge that TNK wanted so badly from VF-Russia.

At that meeting, Jelsma, our president, told Kruger that before any technical knowledge would be shared our team expected TNK to live up to the terms of the joint venture by supplying a timeline for the license transfer — the most important deal point we wanted.

"THEY WANTED TO SHORTCHANGE US BY MILLIONS."

Our attorney, Shelby Bush from Dallas (my son-in-law married to my daughter, Nell,) flew to Moscow just for this meeting. As he began outlining a list of other unresolved issues with TNK, Kruger abruptly and completely out of left field changed the subject of the meeting.

Kruger wanted to discuss the price of renting one of our imported drilling rigs for a TNK project. Hoping to quickly resolve the matter, Jelsma said BaiTex would charge the standard rental price for such a rig in Russia, about $2,000 per day. (In the United States such a rig would lease for $5,000 a day.)

"I will pay $250," Kruger screamed.

The room fell silent as if to absorb the weirdness of the moment.

Then, all hell broke loose for about 10 minutes. Both sides refused to budge on the rental price for the rig, which was not even the subject we were supposed to be talking about.

Slamming his fist on the table, Kruger stood up and shouted, "I am insulted. This meeting is over!"

Like a spoiled teenager, he marched toward the door, opened it and slammed it behind him. The meeting had lasted 15 minutes. Poor Shelby flew all the way to Moscow from Dallas for a 15-minute know-nothing meeting.

Later that afternoon, Kruger, apparently realizing that we were serious about the rental fee amount for the rig — and apparently coming to his senses after letting his anger get the best of him — phoned Yudin in his office. He said he would meet all of us the next day to finalize the terms for the protocol papers required to move all aspects of the BaiTex agreement forward, including the license transfer. Kruger never did agree to our price to rent the drilling rig and we heard no more about it.

When he left the meeting the next day following a pretty good discussion, Kruger still refused to shake hands with any of us or even say goodbye.

"I AM INSULTED. THIS MEETING IS OVER!"

— VICTOR KRUGER

A drilling rig on well No 319, which included the first horizontal leg drilled in the Volga-Ural Basin, Russia.

Applying Pressure

By early May of 2001, no formal papers had been signed, so our back-channel pressure on TNK continued.

Word had filtered up to top management that subordinates had not yet "taken care of business" to make the "pesky American go away." This was a potentially big problem for TNK as it was poised to publicly announce new equity and debt offerings with the backing of U.S. government agencies. TNK could not afford to have these offerings go awry by some small-potato Texan making phone calls to partners in Moscow, London and New York, telling them that a legal matter would ensue if TNK didn't act to honor its contract obligations with a Pioneer Priority Project. A legal issue was the last thing TNK needed now.

In the wild days of the early 1990s, for such pressure tactics against the Russian oligarchs, I might have been taken out of the picture, buried in a shallow grave in some remote Siberian forest or weighted down for a one-way trip to the bottom of a lake near St. Petersburg.

At the very least, hired thugs might have served up a midnight beating to send the message that it was time for the tall Texan to skedaddle back to the safer confines of home.

But in the summer of 2001, I knew their game plan was intimidation masked as hard ball business, so that fear, frustration or both, would make me do what they wanted: pack my bags and retreat from Russia like so many other companies in similar positions had done.

But I did not — and would not.

By now, TNK management had been made clearly aware that with the BaiTex project they had inherited a tempest in a teapot. If I had sued TNK, the manner by which I was being treated and the failure to honor the agreement might have become public. Such publicity undoubtedly would have been embarrassing and, perhaps, led to other unwanted implications at OBN or TNK.

"Contracts were for 'foreigners,' not necessarily Russians."

However, had I sued and won the case, I doubt I would have ever collected a dime, considering the influence of politics on such matters in Russia. The simple fact is that, in those days, contracts were something considered for "foreigners" but not necessarily for Russians. In many cases, I believe the Russians didn't even pay attention to what was in the contracts they signed.

In the fall of 2001 — as the world absorbed the events of the 9-11 attacks — another battle brewed with TNK over the lack of progress to settle the license transfer issue. As storm clouds began building in Moscow, the clouds suddenly began to part — first a little, then a lot.

The drilling floor of a BaiTex well in Russia.

The BaiTex Problem

The continuing pressure we had applied on TNK — including a verbal protest delivered by the U.S. Ambassador to Russia to the President of TNK, Semyon Kukes, at a cocktail party — appeared to be paying off.

In mid-2002, at a meeting of top TNK managers, a member of the team, brought up "the BaiTex problem." The chairman of the meeting exploded in fury. Clearly, he thought the problem had been resolved.

"I'm sick and tired of hearing about this guy Fullinwider and his BaiTex deal!" he said, slamming his fist on the table. "Take care of this deal now. I don't want it coming up on this table anymore. Get out of here and take care of it!"

In short order, I became the problem of TNK's Frank Reiber — and I will be forever grateful I was assigned to his portfolio of responsibilities.

"Frank, do you know this guy, Fullinwider," the TNK manager asked Reiber one day.

"No," Reiber replied.

"Well, this is who he is and here are the numbers he wants. Get with him as quick as you can and get this damn thing worked out," the manager said. "Upper Management doesn't want to hear about it anymore, so just figure it out."

Within a day or so of receiving the assignment, Frank Reiber came to my office. We'd been meeting only about 15 minutes when he said, "These guys have been screwing you for years."

I said, "Well, you're a quick study."

Over the next few months, we and our teams finally drafted an agreement that both sides could live with. We had agreed to a contract in which TNK would pay VF-Neft (neft is the Russian word for oil) — we changed the name of our firm to avoid a new tax on companies using Russia in their names, another silly quirk of doing business in Russia — a substantial portion of the past-due funds owed our firm and accomplish the transfer of the long-awaited license.

As 2002 came to a close, I was hopeful we would finally get the deal done. But, Russia being Russia, I should have known better.

We're just days away from getting the contract approved by TNK's senior management team when their President, without warning, ordered all pending contracts between TNK and any outside party placed on hold, effective immediately. Our agreement was shelved — yet again.

"These guys have been screwing you for years."

— Frank Reiber

CHAPTER 6

MAKING HISTORY

THIS IS GOING TO BE INTERESTING.

Headquartered in London, British Petroleum (BP) is one the world's largest energy companies, operating in more than 80 countries and supplying more than 20,700 service stations worldwide. When word reached me in early 2002 that BP was seriously interested in buying a substantial interest in TNK, I thought to myself, "Well, isn't this going to be interesting." I knew BP was a well-run company and I couldn't help but get excited about a possible opportunity to work with a solid organization.

"I couldn't help but get excited about the opportunity."

BP started in 1909 as the Anglo-Persian Oil Company and became British Petroleum in 1954. Over the years, the company has acquired oil firms and made deals around the world to expand their operations, including an earlier failed venture in Russia. BP was looking to expand its oil reserves; and with Russia having the world's largest untapped oil reserves, they decided to look for another opportunity in Russia.

Taking BP as a suitor was a smart move by TNK, whose hierarchy had accumulated some impressive oilfields and had acquired smaller oil companies since its founding in 1995. But they were not really oil people and needed help to properly manage what they had put together. The TNK hierarchy included some of Russia's top oligarchs. I think these principals thought they could make more money by partnering with a renowned energy expert and granting operational control to BP. Then they could spend their time pursuing other interests.

A Turning Point for BaiTex

What ultimately made TNK attractive to BP was a recent turn around in its production yields — a makeover engineered by Frank Reiber, a third-generation petroleum engineer from California brought in by TNK management to run TNK's field operations and the man negotiating our deal.

Reiber had lived around the world working for large oil companies and small independents, and he was a seasoned and top-notch field development engineer. In Russia, Reiber specialized in picking "low hanging fruit" to improve production yields — these are fairly easy-to-accomplish tasks such as maintaining, modifying or simply cleaning equipment and making needed personnel changes. His efforts in TNK field operations saw production curves shoot up a staggering 300 to 400 percent in a short time. The oil industry around the world took note of TNK's successes; one person who noticed was BP's Group Chief Executive, Lord John Browne.

The pending deal between TNK and BP, that took more than a year to consummate, was the turning point for moving BaiTex out of contractual Purgatory.

BP and TNK struck terms on a deal — a 50-50 partnership that would require an $8 billion buy-in by BP. Months of formal negotiations ensued, and on September 1, 2003, TNK-BP was announced as headline news around the world. Meantime, I struggled to keep the lights on and meet payroll.

Networking to the Top

Lord Browne chose a young geologist named Robert "Bob" Dudley to run TNK-BP. He had been a rising star at Amoco when BP bought the firm some years earlier. Dudley was summoned to Browne's office in London in mid-2003, where he was told to take charge of the ongoing negotiations with TNK. If he was successful, Browne said he would make Dudley president of the new Russian company, TNK-BP.

After learning of Dudley's assignment, I saw an opportunity to meet BP's new man in Russia. He was to be the keynote speaker at an international oil conference at London's Queen Elizabeth II Conference Centre in November 2003. Dudley didn't know me from Adam, and the session was to be attended by more than 1,000 people, but I learned we shared a common school, so I was confident I could get at least a few minutes of his attention — that was all I needed.

"If successful, he was to be president of the new Russian company."

I sat on the front row of the huge auditorium and soaked in the conference. As Dudley's speech ended and he left the podium to large applause, I jumped up from my seat and called to him. Bending down from the stage, Dudley reached to shake my hand as I introduced myself. I knew Bob Dudley had earned a master's degree in business from SMU, so I told him that I was an SMU graduate. I instantly felt a connection, as I believe he did too.

I had my elevator speech ready, and quickly explained to him who I was, the issues I had encountered with TNK and mentioned my attempts to resolve them with the help of Frank Reiber.

"Yes," he said. "I know Frank. He's a good man."

"Yes," I replied. "He's been trying to help me with our problems."

"Are there any problems?" Dudley asked, a genuine tone in his voice.

"Well, you might call them problems. They owe me $5 million, which they've owed for three years, and they can't seem to find the money to pay. And, furthermore, they owe half the income from the oil we've jointly produced, and we haven't heard from that, and they owe this, they owe that, and just won't pay. And, I don't want to get into the court system over this."

By this time, a crowd of people was waiting behind me to talk to Dudley.

He asked, "What's the name of the deal?"

I told him, "BaiTex." I told him a little more, and he took it down on an index card he kept in his shirt pocket.

"Well, I am going to Moscow tomorrow, and I will talk to Frank Reiber. We're going to take care of this."

I could hardly believe my ears. "We're going to take care of this."

"Well," I sputtered. "Wonderful."

I headed back to Moscow the next day, as well. And, sure enough, Frank called me in a few days. "I saw Bob Dudley in the hall. He stopped me and asked me, 'Hey, what's this BaiTex thing?'"

Frank told me he that he proceeded to bring Dudley up to speed on our issues.

"Well, let's get this thing settled," Dudley told Reiber.

" YOU MIGHT CALL THEM PROBLEMS. THEY OWE THIS, THEY OWE THAT, AND JUST WON'T PAY."

Meeting with BP

Two weeks later, while working in my Moscow office, the phone rang. The caller identified himself as Kris Sliger, executive vice president of BP in Moscow. By his name and speech, I surmised he was European. He asked if I would be able to meet with him in his office in two days, which I gladly agreed to.

Young, handsome and impeccably dressed, Sliger was the sort of young executive BP was known to hire. He asked me to bring him up to date on all the facts, and I was delighted to do so. Almost immediately after I finished my initial remarks, Sliger said BP wanted to pay VF-Neft what was owed our firm — an answered prayer, as far as I was concerned.

Then, as I prepared to speak again, Sliger interrupted me.

"Mr. Fullinwider," he began.

I interrupted and said, "Call me Jerry."

"Mr. Fullinwider," he began again, "how are Ann and Sarah?"

My mouth dropped open. Here we were in Moscow, 6,000 miles from Texas and this fellow, an executive vice president of BP with the foreign-sounding name, was asking an intimate family question.

"Ann and Sarah?" I asked, incredulous. "Do you mean my daughters? How do you know my daughters?"

"Mr. Fullinwider, I went to high school with them in Midland, Texas."

Stunned, I almost fell out of my chair. Talk about a small world. Kris said he knew of my reputation — that I was a square guy. We talked about Ann, Sarah and Midland, and when we finished, Kris said he would call me in a couple of days to talk about resolving our problems. I was floored.

Make Us an Offer

A few days later, VF-Neft management met with Sliger and a room full of BP lawyers. The mood was serious.

"Mr. Fullinwider," Sliger began, "wouldn't it be more convenient if you owned the entire joint venture?"

What did he just ask? My mind raced.

"It would really be a whole lot easier on you," he said. "You wouldn't have to talk to us about anything — not budgets, or wells you wanted to drill. You could drill when and where you want to. You wouldn't have to give us production schedules, reports or anything. You know, it'd really be a whole lot easier on you if you owned the whole thing. Why don't you buy our share from us?"

I sat a moment, in disbelief, trying hard not to show it.

To myself, I said, "There is something else here that they're saying, or, rather, not saying. There is more to this than meets the eye."

I spoke. "Kris, look," I said. "I've been over here 15 years and haven't made a dime. I've spent a ton of money — way too much of my own money, and I've only met with grief. I'm not really interested in spending more money to acquire your one-half interest."

I paused. "I can't afford it. I just don't have the funds," I said.

"Just make us an offer," Sliger said. "You don't have to spend a lot of money. Just make us an offer. When we get out of this deal, you'll have the whole thing to yourself. That will take care of it."

My mind raced.

"Just make us an offer," Sliger repeated.

"I've only met with grief."

I'm One of the Liabilities

I realized what was going on. At least I thought I did. By extending this olive branch, BP was observing in an unspoken way that they had inherited a contractual obligation the subsequent TNK brass had failed to pay. In addition, OBN had failed to pay approximately $50 million in past oil revenue. BP didn't want that to come up.

By the end of the meeting, the puzzle came together. BP knew that OBN had breached the joint venture agreement. TNK had innocently bought that huge liability when it acquired OBN. TNK owed us at least $5 million for field development and we had the papers to prove it. In Russia, if you pay for anything, you must have contractual papers substantiating the work done and the payment for such work.

TNK-BP was in a box, even though it was not the company's fault. This was a can of worms no one wanted to open. TNK-BP wanted this liability to go away.

"You know guys," I said, as the meeting concluded. "I know this is not your doing. You're trying to clean it up, and I want to be helpful. But you bought the assets and you also bought the liabilities, and I'm one of the liabilities."

Sliger and the room full of BP lawyers nodded their heads in agreement.

"You bought the assets and you also bought the liabilities."

My First Offer

I offered to buy out TNK-BP's 50 percent share of the BaiTex operation for $1 million — $1 million for an oilfield of about 80 million barrels of recoverable oil worth probably at least 200 times that amount. That was the amount of money I felt fairly confident that I could raise on my own, and, of course, it would have been a pretty good deal — a hell of a deal, if the offer was accepted.

"Jerry, this is not a serious offer," Sliger told me upon hearing it.

"Well, you said just make me an offer."

"And, yes, I did, but we can't do that."

I told Sliger, "Well, let me think about it."

159

Jerry meets with British investor Tom Vallance and an associate at the Baituganskoye field and outlines his next moves.

Figuring Out a Reasonable Offer

Over the next few days, with the help of my team, we ran some numbers based on some conservative assumptions, factoring in what we were owed, discounts on future valuations and the eagerness with which the motivated seller wanted out of the joint venture. We arrived at a purchase price taking into account the forgiveness of their $5.0 million debt and the past monies owed for our half of the oil revenue.

Leah was worried. She didn't want me to spend one more dime of our money in Russia.

"Jerry," Leah said, "where are we going to get that kind of money. If you borrow it, at your age you may not be able to pay it back. We might lose our home."

I was just about tapped out of money, to be sure. Fifteen years of investment, paying for equipment, salaries, lawyers, travel, upkeep and expenses for residences in Moscow and Texas with almost no revenue coming in had just about broken me.

But I didn't have any choice but to borrow the money from a bank or with the help of yet more investors. None of the options appealed to me.

"I didn't have any choice but to borrow money— I was tapped out."

Finding the Funds

At about this time, August of 2004, my son-in-law — Sarah's husband — had arrived in Russia for a long-planned trip to see the Baituganskoye oilfield. Ever since he had been to Russia on his first trip a year earlier, he had been asking me to take him to the oilfield for an up-close tour.

Ross Perot Jr. is a father-in-law's best wish for his daughter; he is a smart, successful businessman, a wonderful husband and a terrific father. Ross serves as Chairman of the Perot Group, which manages the various Perot family interests that include real estate, oil and gas and financial investments.

Ross's first trip to Russia in 2004 included a celebration dinner for leading Russian executives at the excellent restaurant "Imperial" in Moscow; they even put out the Texas flag.

After a driving excursion around the BaiTex field, Ross and I boarded a helicopter and toured the surrounding areas by air before proceeding to the little island in the small, spring-fed lake that was the centerpiece of the oilfield. There, we enjoyed a picnic attended by our Russian field staff, the mayor of the nearest village, the local fire chief and other local VIPs.

Per their customary hospitality, the women of the village prepared a delicious feast that included Russian shish kabob, vegetables and homemade pastries. We drank wine, sipped vodka, sang songs and toasted our mutual friendships and successes.

During the festivities, Ross turned to me and said, "I'm impressed with what you're doing here. You really know these people. I'd like to get in on this deal. Do you need any money?"

Did I need any money? Always!

Startled by the offer, I told Ross that I had plans to pursue funds from British investors who were interested in backing us.

"Well, why bring another party in? Let's keep it in the family." he said, tendering an offer I could not refuse.

I said, "Great!" I meant it. I didn't want to have to fool with a bunch of London lawyers and their paperwork. We made a simple deal on the spot.

"AN 80-MILLION-
BARREL OILFIELD
IS NO BIG DEAL
IN RUSSIA."

Jerry at the office of TNK-BP with his son-in-law and partner Ross Perot Jr.; Bob Dudley, president/CEO of TNK-BP; and Valery Yudin, to complete the buyout of BaiTex's Russian partner OBN, December 2004.

A Done Deal

In West Texas, if I had made a deal as a Texas independent oilman to own outright an oilfield with 80 million barrels of recoverable oil, my picture would be on the cover of *Time* magazine. But when TNK-BP accepted my offer to purchase their 50 percent share of BaiTex in August of 2004, there was no publicity — and none was wanted. Besides, an 80-million-barrel oilfield is no big deal in Russia.

At the moment the agreement was signed, TNK-BP transferred the license. VF-Neft — Leah and I, along with our family and our faithful group of small investors — had become, as far as we know, the first Western company in history to hold 100 percent ownership of a Russian oilfield.

After 15 years of warfare (or so it often felt), the history of the moment did not escape me.

And, the milestone in Russian history did not escape my Russian friends.

"Jerry, this is historic!" said my friend Valery Garipov, a deputy minister in the Russian Oil and Gas Ministry, when I visited his office a few weeks later.

"Yes, I know, because it's taken me so damned long to try to work this deal out," I replied.

"No, that's not what we're all talking about," the deputy minister said. "Do you not understand? No major Russian oil company has ever sold an oilfield to a Western company. This is the first time that it has ever happened. And now, you own 100 percent of it!"

"Yes, but how long will I own it?" I asked, intending the question to be taken literally. I had elaborate plans to fully develop the BaiTex field, using new technology to improve production; to employ more Russians; to enjoy Russia's beauty, arts and music for years to come — but I also knew those plans carried great risk because of a force I could not influence easily, let alone control.

"We know President Putin has been speaking a lot about how he doesn't want Westerners coming to take hold of strategic stakes in the oil business. Is our owning 100 percent of an oilfield going to be a problem?"

The deputy minister paused, looked at me thoughtfully and said, "We don't know. It might be a problem."

I was not surprised by the honest answer.

"Is our owning 100 percent of an oilfield going to be a problem?"

CHAPTER 7

COMING HOME

PUTIN WAS ADAMANT ABOUT NOT GRANTING STRATEGIC HOLDINGS IN THE RUSSIAN OIL FIELDS TO FOREIGNERS.

Putin served as President of Russia from 2000 to 2008 and again beginning in May 2012. He was Prime Minister of Russia from 1999 to 2000 and again from 2008 to 2012. Before that, Putin was a longtime officer in the KGB, rising to become the head of the KGB's successor, the FSB, in 1997.

"I worried about someone coming along and taking over."

Putin has made no secret of his belief that energy is the basis of Russia's geopolitical bargaining power — and that oil and gas should stay under Kremlin control. He wrote his doctoral thesis on the topic: "The Strategic Planning of Regional Resources Under the Formation of Market Relations," which argued the importance of establishing national energy champions to ensure the economic success of Russia. Putin saw the importance of Russia having so many natural resources, including oil; and he knew these resources could be used to expand Russia's power. I read his thesis and his tenure as president of Russia was right in line with it, point by point.

Under Putin's rule, oligarchs and the drama that came with them continued to be a problem.

We were worried because Putin was adamant about not granting to foreigners strategic holdings in the Russian oil fields. At any given time, operations were shut down if someone of power wanted them to be; the government would find an environmental issue or problems with bank loans, taxes, or really anything to take over a project.

Although the Baituganskoye oilfield was considered small, I knew we had a nice, clean oilfield and I worried about someone coming along and finding a way to take it over. It had taken me nearly 16 years to obtain the ownership and control of the field. Keeping it was no longer the question. The questions now were when to sell — and to whom?

Preparing for the Sale

Bob Foresman, who then led investment banking in Russia for Germany's Dresdner Bank AG, and a good friend and expert banker, laid out my options. It was January of 2005 and I could sell the Russian operation within the next eight months before Russia's election season began which would effectively stop business deals from being made. Otherwise, I would need to wait several years to see who would become the new Russian president, what his policies will be toward foreign ownership of oil properties and how close he was to Putin.

"Jerry, you either sell within the next year or you may have to wait about five years, until the next election cycle has been completed. By then we will know who the next president is going be," said Bob, whom I also knew as an elder at the Moscow church that Leah and I attended. Bob was also a devoted husband to his Russian wife and wonderful father to his five children. Our two families shared a deep love of family, religion, music and the arts.

"Golly," I said. "I don't want to wait five years to figure out what might happen next, so let's get it on and get it sold before Mr. Putin figures out that a Western company owns 100 percent of an oilfield on his turf. Not that he would ever care for such a little field, but I don't want to run that risk."

Foresman recommended that we sell the company through a private auction. In a private auction, prospective bidders are handpicked and pre-qualified, and they have registered an interest in acquiring Russian oil properties. Bidders are contacted privately and, in confidence, sent a prospectus on the property for sale and invited to submit an "indicative price" for which they might purchase the property. But such indicative price would not be a "firm offer" which was to be settled later.

We brought in Dallas-based petroleum consultants DeGolyer-MacNaughton, whose experts I had tapped at the beginning of my Russian adventure. Their job was to evaluate the reserves in the Baituganskoye field and assess the value of our equipment, our future production and all the rest, so we could set a realistic and competitive price. The valuation process took six months. Along the way, we contracted with KPMG, the global accounting firm, to audit our books, and we prepared a formal prospectus on the property; those two huge tasks took another six months. And finally, we couldn't have completed the sale without the council of the venerable Akin Gump law firm. Their guidance was paramount to our success in these negotiations.

Jerry, right, and Bob Foresman, the banker who helped close the deal with Hungary's state-owned MOL Group.

The Auction

As I was well aware, there was always unpredictable risk when doing business in Russia. The sale of an oil property would require involvement of the Russian tax police, the Anti-Monopoly Committee (ostensibly established to ensure fair business practices), a slew of regulatory and environmental agencies that would have to sign off on the deal, and there was the potential threat of political intervention at any juncture of the deal process.

By late fall of 2005, we were ready to go to market with the BaiTex project. Immediately, we had four good "lookers," although one fell out fast. We invited the three remaining firms to examine our records, equipment, production projections and, of course, the BaiTex field and facilities. One firm withdrew shortly thereafter, citing a desire to concentrate their oil investments at home. Later, the second firm withdrew its interest, scared off by Mr. Putin's increasingly nationalistic speeches regarding foreigners in his oil patch. That left one firm. Of course, none of the firms knew who their potential competitors might be or which of the firms may have dropped out of the running. We had to hold out hope that Putin's rhetoric would not escalate before the sale could be closed.

"I FELT THE PRESSURE TO MAKE A DEAL."

The Agreement with MOL

MOL Group is the state-owned oil company of Hungary, and, as we would soon learn, was not to be scared off by anyone — including Mr. Putin. MOL is the biggest company in Hungary, run by some of the brightest executives.

MOL had been under pressure to increase its energy holdings in Eastern Europe and in Russia to ensure stable sources of energy for Hungary's growing economy. The previous year, the Hungarian government had allotted $1 billion or more toward the purchase of energy assets. By the time our company had gone on the market, MOL had spent almost none of its allotted funds and was under pressure to make things happen.

After looking into our operations, MOL was impressed by the above-reproach advisors we used, as well as our open approach to business. I was able to answer their questions and openly share details about our company.

I also felt the pressure to make a deal with only one bidder still in the running.

"Pray for your Dad," Leah wrote in an email to our daughter, Ann. "He has his second meeting with the competing companies and will give them the proposed selling price which he is willing to take for the oilfield. The meeting is tomorrow afternoon. The bank handling sale proceedings told him this is the first time that they have allowed a CEO to do his own negotiations, but he is so on top of everything with figures, facts and background that they could not possibly do as well as he does. Nice compliment."

In the end, MOL offered a fair price for BaiTex.

I had invested nearly 16 years of my life into the project. For this investment, we stood to get our original investment back plus a handsome profit. Not a bad deal, I figured even with the usual deductions of bank and legal fees, taxes, closing costs and investors' share.

So we agreed to sell to MOL Group.

The Closing Ceremony

As we drew up the sales papers that were subject to approval by the Russian bureaucracy at any time if it so desired, I told Foresman that I wanted the deal closed in Budapest, for strategic reasons to avoid possible Russian bureaucracy interference.

The Hungarians agreed to my desire, but they recommended another location for making the deal, pending funding: the Hungarian Embassy in Moscow's famous Sparrow Hills district, located in the hills high above Moscow's summertime heat and air pollution.

Sparrow Hills includes the huge Moscow State University campus, tree-lined boulevards and panoramic views of Moscow.

The Hungarian Embassy is situated on sovereign Hungarian territory — not Russian soil. In short order, both parties had received an invitation from Hungarian Ambassador Arpad Svekely to consummate the deal at the Hungarian Embassy in early December 2006.

I'll never forget the morning we arrived at the Embassy. Ambassador Svekely, beyond excited, greeted us like long lost relatives. Dressed in his formal ambassadorial attire — he had a blue satin ribbon draped across his chest — he shook our hands and urged us to partake of his hospitality. As a band played a series of classical marches on the front porch, servants with white gloves brought us champagne, vodka, cognac or other drinks of our choice. An elaborate spread of caviar, little sandwiches, crackers, cheeses and other hors d'oeuvres was set up for us to partake. The band, the food, the ambassador — it was a scene out of movie; probably one like it had been filmed nearby.

We signed the papers — save the few signatures each party would make at closing once funds were transferred — and stood together to smile for photos taken by the court photographer. We toasted each other with vodka, chatted with the ambassador and had a grand time.

Ferenc, the team leader of the MOL Group, at the deal selling BaiTex to MOL Group at the Hungarian Embassy in Moscow, December 2006.

Officially Closing the Deal

Now, it was time to close the deal.

I very much wanted to close before the end of the year to accomodate some charitable gifts to come of our favorite causes. I had suggested to the Hungarian buyers that we close the deal in Budapest. When I learned that the buyers said they could close the deal anywhere, I suggested London — neutral ground.

The closing would work this way: the buyers would open an account with J.P. Morgan in London into which they would deposit funds to purchase the BaiTex project; I would open a parallel account at J.P. Morgan to receive the funds. The bank would alert me when the buyer's account is funded with the monies to close; both parties then would meet together at J.P. Morgan's London headquarters to exchange and sign closing documents and oversee the transfer of funds from the buyer's account to ours.

At noon on Thursday, December 28, 2006, with one business day of the year to spare, representatives from MOL Group, members of our group, including Leah, and several bankers from J.P. Morgan gathered on the 14th floor of the London headquarters of J.P. Morgan in the financial district to close the sale of BaiTex.

I was on the verge of closing the largest deal of my oil career.

With the papers of sale spread out on the table — as yet unsigned — the banker assigned to work with me showed me a computer screen placed in front of me with two accounts displayed: the buyer's account with the exact amount of purchase funds in place, and my account, which was empty.

Both parties signed the closing sale documents and posed for a few photographs. Then, the final sales transaction was made. As I watched the computer screen, I saw the funds that had been in the buyer's account almost instantaneously appear in my account. The sale to MOL Group was complete, but I wasn't done on my end. I gave the banker another account number and said, "Please wire the funds to this account in Dallas." He did so, and then we had to wait a long two-and-a-half hours for confirmation that the funds had been received. With the money safely in Texas, I said a prayer to myself. "Thank you, Lord."

The business press reported the sale of BaiTex to MOL Group on Friday, December 29, 2006.

Leah reported the sale to our family and friends in a joyful email from London. "We have sold our Russian oil company!" Leah wrote. "It has been many months in the working — hard to believe it is done. JMF and I are sad to say goodbye to so many faithful employees in Russia from the past 16 years, but feel strongly it is the right time to leave Russia and receive this as a chapter ending by God's gracious provision."

BAITEX SOLD TO MOL GROUP

BUDAPEST, Dec. 29 (Reuters) — Hungarian oil and gas group MOL said on Friday it has bought a Russian oilfield operator, in a deal analysts said was relatively small but fits well with MOL's strategy.

MOL bought oil firm BaiTex LLC from U.S.-based VF-NEFT Development LLC. BaiTex owns the license to the subsoil under the Baituganskoye oil producing field in the Volgal-Ural region, one of Russia's main oil producing provinces.

Farewell Celebrations

Bidding farewell to the oilfield workers was bittersweet. Two weeks before the sale closed, Leah joined me and the management team for a trip to Buguruslan, the city nearest the BaiTex field, to celebrate the pending sale, and so I could say my goodbyes to the field employees and managers.

As is the tradition in Russia, we had several layers of celebration. The first was a private lunch at a hotel with the field managers and supervisors who had done such an outstanding job turning the field around. After a great meal, I toasted them, and with the help of Viktor, my interpreter, spoke a few words and thanked them for their hard work. Then, I told them that under their place settings, they would find an envelope with their name on it. Inside, was a formal note of thanks and the bonus amount each would receive when the BaiTex deal closed. The room full of managers sat still and smiled. They did not make any motion to open their envelopes. I asked Viktor if he accurately conveyed the message. He replied that he had done so.

"Well, tell them to open their blasted envelopes," I told Viktor. I wanted the joy of seeing their faces when they did.

I never had so much fun watching a group of people in all my life. Faces lit up with broad smiles; others stared in disbelief; others appeared on the verge of tears. Bonuses of such large amounts — the minimum being a year's salary — were unheard of for Russian employees, let alone oilfield employees.

Jerry hosted a meal with BaiTex's Russian employees to celebrate the company's sale to the Hungarians. They were so moved they got up to say: "greatest thing you brought us was hope" and one woman spoke about how wonderful it had been to work with our company and get paid on time!

"Tell them to open their blasted envelopes."

Later that afternoon, a similar scene played out in a large auditorium at which the 175 rank-and-file employees and their families gathered for a company potluck supper that was organized as a thank you to me. As usual, the Russian women had cooked all kinds of wonderful foods and prepared beautiful table settings with white linen napkins.

Following the wonderful homemade feast, I was presented two gifts: handmade desk ornaments — oil derricks — that were inscribed with the date, the name of the oilfield and a personal inscription, all in Russian. I knew you couldn't buy such a gift in local stores, and I was very moved when I received it.

Just as I did in the meeting with the field managers, I told the employees gathered in the auditorium how much I appreciated their hard work and what good employees they were, how they had turned the oilfield around and given new life to the area. I will never forget them, I said.

The handmade gifts presented to Jerry at the company celebration.

"I've never seen such a happy group of human beings."

Then, I proceeded to tell them that each employee would receive an envelope with a special thank you from me for their service along with a notification of a bonus each would receive once the company sale was completed. When I spoke the word bonus, a look of confusion overcame the faces of employees, and some faces registered worry as if the letters were layoff notices.

"Now, the superintendents and other bosses will get more bonus than the others, but everybody will get a bonus, including the women cleaning the bathrooms," I said, their faces registering more disbelief when Viktor translated the word bathroom as "cleaning toilets."

"I won't tell you what the largest bonus will be," I continued, "but I will tell you what the smallest bonus will be for everybody, and that is one year's salary in one payment."

Well, they didn't understand what I had just said.

I told Viktor to explain what a bonus is and what each employee would receive.

When he did, the room erupted. I've never seen such a happy group of human beings. This wasn't done in Russia. They looked at each other and said words to the effect, "This can't be real."

Then the real party began. Before I realized what was under way, I was escorted to the dance floor by a plump Russian woman; Leah was right behind me, being led, I presumed, by the woman's equally plump Russian husband. The vodka flowed.

Saying Goodbye

Finally, it was time to say goodbye. Leah captured the moment in an email home to our family and friends.

"They gave him a standing ovation, not because of the promised bonus but I could tell because they were really sad to tell him good-bye. There was evidence of tears and emotions. I don't think those workers have ever been treated with respect and courtesy the way they have been these past 15 years (plus the steady paychecks).

"Many of them are there because their parents and grandparents have worked in those oilfields for the past 38 to 50 years. That is the only life they have ever known. BaiTex has helped several young men get some education and they have come back as engineers and computer experts.

"We thought this trip would be important for the company employees, but as it progressed it became apparent to me that this was of greatest benefit to JMF. He is having a hard time walking away from this huge chapter in his life. I could tell he was in a grief process when I arrived (a few days earlier)…I assured him that this was a normal and expected response on his part. He had not realized that (grief) was going on and seemed comforted. (At the final goodbye,) hearing the thanks and appreciation (of the company personnel) for him was such a healing balm. He realizes that this is where his success really lies more than monetary results of selling the company."

And, Leah was right.

On the morning of Saturday, December 30, Leah and I boarded a plane at London's Heathrow airport for our trip back to Dallas. We were eager to start the year 2007 with another big celebration — this one with family — and back in our territory, Texas.

Before we left London, I reflected with our banker, Bob Foresman, on how smoothly the sale of BaiTex had gone in the course of just a few weeks. We had escaped the obstacles that could have arisen — the Russian bureaucracy, the specter of political intervention and other potential roadblocks. After 16 years of struggle we had finally succeeded.

CHAPTER 8

THINKING AHEAD OF THE CROWD

NEVER GIVE UP.

As best I know, no person in U.S. history has accomplished what I was able to do in the oil business, beginning in 1989 under the government of the Soviet Union, and concluding in 2006, under the government of Russia. I wish to tell this story to other entrepreneurs with big dreams, so that they might learn from my experience — to never give up, to jump on the right deal, to wait on the better deal, to confront bullies head on, and to persevere when every other competitor is bailing out because of hardship or impatience.

"I wanted to satisfy my deep curiosity."

Most all of my friends — and my wife on more than one occasion — considered me nuts for investing so much time, energy and money into pursuing a business where one like it had never existed before. Few people believed me when I told them that I had not gone to the former Soviet Union with the intention of getting into the oil business. I had concocted no grand plan to "strike it rich."

I went there, initially, because I had been invited; I wanted to be helpful to the Soviet oil officials who hosted me and who — despite our language, cultural and political differences — were as passionate as I about the oil business. I wanted to satisfy my deep curiosity about a people and a place whose economic way of life I held strong pre-conceived opinions. And maybe I wanted to engage in some business. Russia possessed all of these qualities at just the right time in my life and, perhaps, at the right time for Russia. In retrospect, I got more than I bargained for — and, improbably, perhaps more than I deserved.

It Has Never Been Boring

When I think of the sheer improbability of my Russian adventure, I am reminded of the old canard, "Do you know how to make God laugh?"

"Tell him your plans."

I wish I could say that I had this wonderful plan to succeed in the Russian oilfield, with everything all laid out perfectly, so it would proceed like clockwork. But I didn't have any plan at all. I operated week to week, asking myself, "Are you going to stay in this deal or not?" But through the grace of God, doors just kept opening in Russia, and I just kept walking through them.

Another reason I embarked on this improbable journey, I must confess, is my lifelong itch to learn, or maybe just to be entertained. New places and situations attract me more than just about anything. I am controlled, too often, I admit, by my naiveté that everything will work out just dandy. When I played my trumpet in the dance band, my greatest fun came from sight reading. Would I be able to stay up with the other players? Could I hit a high D that appeared with no warning? It is coping with the unknown that provides me a sense of creativity. It is energizing to wonder what might happen next!

When Leah is asked about living life with me, her standard reply is, "Well, it has never been boring."

Leah and I celebrated our 57th wedding anniversary on March 17, 2014.

Reflecting on my time in Russia, I probably should have been committed.

Jerry and Leah attending the Tzar's Ball, a gala in St. Petersburg.

Life Lessons Learned

BE CURIOUS

I'm often asked, "Jerry, what are some of the lessons you learned about doing business in Russia?" Talk about a loaded question.

First, go in with eyes wide-open. Do your research — carefully. While I did a little scientific research with Ward Austin to prepare for my adventure, I mainly threw myself into learning everything I could about Russia. I did my due diligence by reading anything I could find about the oil industry in Russia and Russia itself; I definitely had to read outside my comfort zone.

Being in the oil industry myself, I was fascinated by the Russians and what they were doing in the oil industry and the potential for future growth. I have a huge curiosity for life, and I am certain that my curiosity and fascination with the industry helped me succeed in Russia. I was amazed that I possessed knowledge that they did not have, but wanted and needed. I thrived on being able to share my expertise with these powerful Russian businessmen.

An oil storage tank at Baituganskoye bears the BaiTex logo.

"Open your heart, but be prepared to have it wounded."

FIND ALLIES

Don't rely on only one domestic partner to provide local contacts and influence. In Russia, a foreigner could never hope to do more than scratch the surface in terms of local knowledge and influence. One can never fully understand their culture so it is important to align yourself with those who are native to the culture. You need to establish a local network of influence — local political and business leaders.

A key to my success, ultimately, was growing my own network of contacts and keeping them informed as to what I was doing and the value I was bringing to Russia. Trust and personal relationships were key in my surviving and, eventually, thriving. Who you know — not what you know — is what counts in Russia. It was critical that I meet the people I needed to know and avoided those I did not need to know in Russia. Open your heart, but be prepared to have it wounded from time to time.

LIFE LESSONS LEARNED

- ⊙ Go in with eyes wide open.
- ⊙ Do your research carefully.
- ⊙ Read outside your comfort zone.
- ⊙ Maintain a huge curiosity for life.
- ⊙ Align yourself with natives.
- ⊙ Build a local network of influence.
- ⊙ Open your heart, but be prepared.
- ⊙ Share your blessings.
- ⊙ Think ahead of the crowd.
- ⊙ Nothing is ever as it appears.

SHARE YOUR BLESSINGS

Also, when you succeed, share your blessings. On one occasion, to pass time on a long flight between Russia and Dallas — and to keep my hopes up during another tough time — I made a list of 10 organizations that I would like to give $1 million each. I didn't know whether I would be able to follow through, but it was my intention. During a particularly rough patch in Russia, I crumpled up the list and threw it away. "Oh, you dreamer," I remember telling myself. "You haven't gotten a dime out of Russia and probably never will."

But on the flight back to Dallas from London on the day after we closed the sale of the BaiTex operation, I made a new list of organizations we would give gifts of $1 million each. This time I came up with a list of 12 organizations. It was pure fun to call each of the recipients. They couldn't believe it. The making of the money wasn't always so much fun but giving some of it away brought great joy. In a sense, it was payback for all the abuse along the way.

"I SEEMED TO POSSESS A MISSIONARY SPIRIT."

THINK AHEAD OF THE CROWD

Once, a newswoman asked me if I had a "business motto" that describes my approach to commerce. I thought about her question before replying. In fact, I thought back through the milestones of my life, my career in oil and my overall approach to everyday matters. I came up with a phrase that fits pretty well: "Think ahead of the crowd."

The modern Russian oil industry began with the creation of the first vertically-integrated companies in 1992 — companies such as LUKoil, Surgutneftegaz, YUKOS and Rosneft (then and now controlled by the Russian government). I thought ahead of the crowd, when I formed VF-Russia, Inc. in 1990 — two years earlier.

The fact that I even went to Russia was thinking ahead of the crowd. Very few of my peers had given any thought about going there to be involved in the oil industry. Most thought it was absurd that I was planning to go. Similar to my great-great-grandfather, I seemed to possess a missionary spirit, which I used hand-in-hand with my entrepreneurial bent throughout my time in Russia. I was willing to help even when, at that time, no other western company would. I loved sharing my knowledge and being of help to the Russian people I met along the way. I have spent my life serving God, my family and others, and my time in Russia was another opportunity for me to give and share what God has blessed me with.

From the moment I heard him speak the words while I was yet a boy, I adopted the philosophy spoken by Gen. Douglas MacArthur: "There is no security on this Earth — only opportunity."

Faced with ominous threats and set back after set back, why didn't I simply pack for home right then? If truth be told, I had made good friends in Russia, and I had become enamored by the music, arts and culture. Some years before, I had already made the decision, although later wobbly at times, that I would stick it out in Russia, until I played my last hand or was forced to fold. I thought I had reached that point in Russia on many an occasion, only to find a new card — or be granted one, miracle-like — in order to keep my enterprise afloat.

I would face the enemy, whatever setback, new regulation or bureaucrat was blocking progress, or I would go out trying. Yet, I had no illusions about Russia. There is nothing on my birth certificate, on my high school or college diplomas, on my Navy Commission or on my passport that guaranteed I would be a business success in Russia — nothing.

As setback after setback occurred, I was determined to find a solution. I was always looking for handles to stay alive business-wise and physically. As one solution fell through, I was always prepared with another option, constantly finding something that would work. Frequent changes in laws and leadership caused us to operate in a state of flux. Through it all, I had to stand patient and adaptable as I struggled to stay afloat in Russia.

I pressed on with boldness, tenacity, integrity and strength. And I was enabled to persevere to the end. By the grace of God and with the support of my family, I came home from Russia making business history and with a changed heart for Russia.

You know, in Russia they say nothing is ever as it appears. And I guess the same could be said about me. Here I am, a conservative, Texas oilman who gained not only historical business accomplishments in Russia but lifelong Russian friends, something no one, including myself, would have ever expected.

"Nothing is ever as it appears, including me."

Jerry's Who's Who

BAITEX

The company Jerry set up for the joint venture deal with OBN for the Baituganskoye field. OBN's portion of the BaiTex joint venture was later transferred to TNK, when TNK bought OBN.

BRITISH PETROLEUM — BP

One of the largest energy companies in the world.

MD SEIS

The first U.S.-Soviet joint venture for oil exploration and production started by Tom Russell.

MOL GROUP

The Hungarian-owned oil ompany that purchased BaiTex.

ORENBURGNEFT — OBN
The Russian-owned company that Jerry set up his joint venture with. OBN was bought by TNK.

PROFESSIONAL GEOPHYSICS, INC. — PGI
The Houston firm led by Tom Russell.

STANDARD OIL OF OHIO
Jerry's first job in the oil industry was with SOHIO in Houston.

Jerry's Who's Who

TNK-BP

BP's Russian operation and TNK merged to create TNK-BP to handle Russian oil operations. TNK-BP took over TNK's portion of the BaiTex joint venture. TNK-BP eventually sold their share of the Baituganskoye field to BaiTex.

TYUMEN OIL COMPANY OF WESTERN SIBERIA — TNK

One of Russia's largest privately-owned companies, which bought out OBN.

VF-NEFT

When Russia established a 1% throughput tax for any company using Russia in its name, Jerry changed the name of VF-Russia to VF-Neft.

V-F PETROLEUM

Jerry's first independent oil company based in Midland, Texas, was started with partner, Vic Vasicek.

VF-RUSSIA

The parent company of BaiTex that Jerry started originally at the advice of his accountant so he could attach expenses from his early Russia research and visits to a specific company; it later became VF-Neft.

WHERE ARE THEY NOW?

Sadly, I've already had to say goodbye to many great friends who played such key roles in my russian adventure. **Ward Austin, Tom Russell, Frank Reiber and Nicholi Lisovsky** all died early due to illness.

"Sadly, I've already had to say goodbye to many great friends."

Bryan Aldridge, the entrepreneurially-minded oil and gas attorney who assisted me greatly on my Russian adventure, remains in private practice, and is one of Texas' leading petroleum industry lawyers.

Valery Yudin is retired and happily enjoying country life in his dacha surrounded by adoring grandchildren.

Viktor Nikitin continues to consult for U.S. and Russian companies as a world-class translator and interpreter.

Henk Jelsma has developed a thriving oilfield services firm with offices in both Russia and Houston.

Peter Postojenko is a highly-sought geologic consultant in Russia, a top specialist in the Orenburg Oblast [Volga-Urals basin].

Valery Garipov is a geophysical consultant in Moscow, working with both independent and major oil firms.

Alexie Kashik, who worked so closely with us as General Director of the Central Geophyiscal Expedition in Moscow, remains active at CGE and also in his position as a Director of the Russian Academy of Sciences.

Bob Foresman, a great friend and banker, is now managing director of the Russian operation of Barclays, the British multinational banking and financial services company headquartered in London. Bob is also on the board of directors of TMK, Russia's largest pipemaker, which speaks volumes about the respect he has among Russian business and political hierarchy.

Vitaly Tkachev continues to ply his services as a consultant to Russian oil firms. Once, I told Frank Reiber the story of how Tkachev essentially threatened our operations, if not our lives, if we didn't sign our operations over to TNK. Reiber said, "Oh, that guy is a pushover. He's a big blowhard. I hope you didn't pay any attention to him." Frank told me later that he ran into Tkachev and told Tkachev what my perception of the meeting was that day in Tkachev's office. "He (Tkachev) just laughed," Reiber said.

Irina Kapina remained our office manager in Moscow until 2013. She and our accountant there, Kolya Ulianov, were the last employees of our only remaining Russian company, VF-Neft Development, LLC, which we permanently closed in 2013, following the sale of our office building.

And, finally, my dear friend, George Gogonenkov. George also continues his position as Senior First Deputy Director of Central Geophysical Expedition in Moscow. When not in Moscow, he enjoys his country *dacha* and time with his grandchildren. George expected nothing from me and never asked for a dime for his advice. On my last trip to Russia, George hugged me deeply and cried. I did too.

A BaiTex well in the Soksoye field.

WWW.EPICBOUNDBOOKS.COM

(210) 373-9313

Publication Director: Rory W. Siefer

Creative Director: Ali Abercrombie

Graphic Designer: Jacq Davis

Executive Editor: Traci Chandler

Copy Editor: Gerard MacCrossan

Printed in the USA